CAMBRIDGE CONTEXTS IN LITERATURE

The Age of Chaucer

Valerie Allen

Series Editor: Adrian Barlow

CAMBRIDGE
UNIVERSITY PRESS

PUBLISHED BY THE PRESS SYNDICATE OF THE UNIVERSITY OF CAMBRIDGE
The Pitt Building, Trumpington Street, Cambridge, United Kingdom

CAMBRIDGE UNIVERSITY PRESS
The Edinburgh Building, Cambridge CB2 2RU, UK
40 West 20th Street, New York, NY 10011-4211, USA
477 Williamstown Road, Port Melbourne, VIC 3207, Australia
Ruiz de Alarcón 13, 28014 Madrid, Spain
Dock House, The Waterfront, Cape Town 8001, South Africa

http://www.cambridge.org

First published 2004

Printed in the United Kingdom at the University Press, Cambridge

Typefaces: Clearface and Mixage   *System:* QuarkXpress® 4.04

A catalogue record for this book is available from the British Library

ISBN 0 521 52993X paperback
Prepared for publication by Liz Paren
Designed by Tattersall Hammarling & Silk
Cover photography: Picking cherries (vellum) by Italian School, (14th century)
courtesy of Bridgeman Art Library, London / Osterreichische Nationalbibliothek,
Vienna, Austria

Acknowledgements

The author and publishers wish to thank the following for permission to use copyright material:

Blackwell Publishing for material from Derek Pearsall, ed. *From Chaucer to Spenser* (1999);
Faber and Faber Ltd and WW Norton & Company, Inc for an extract from Seamus Heaney,
Beowulf. Copyright © 2000 by Seamus Heaney; Houghton Mifflin Company for material from
The Riverside Chaucer, 3rd edition, Larry D Benson, General Editor. Copyright © 1987 by
Houghton Mifflin Company; Oxford University Press for extracts from 'Saddlers Play' and 'Fishers
and Mariners Play' from *York Mystery Plays: A Selection in Modern Spelling,* eds Richard Beadle
and Pamela M King (1984) pp. 241, 24-5.

Every effort has been made to trace the copyright holders; the publishers would like to hear from
anyone whose rights they have unknowingly infringed.

Contents

Introduction

The medieval world, in particular the fourteenth century, has inspired artists, architects, designers and writers, and fascinated audiences for more than six hundred years. Pre-Raphaelite paintings, neo-Gothic railway stations and reworkings of the Arthurian legends are all evidence of ways in which the medieval captured the imagination of later ages. Culturally, historically and linguistically that world may seem impossibly distant from our own. This book explores the world in which Chaucer wrote; it offers opportunities for comparison between his work and that of his near contemporaries; and discusses stylistic variations to be found between Chaucer and other writers, and within Chaucer's own texts.

The society which shaped the texts

C.S. Lewis pointed out, in his *Studies in Medieval and Renaissance Literature,* that books from the past can be appreciated far more if we approach them with a deeper and fuller understanding of the world in which they were written. A superficial reader, he said, is like a tourist who 'carries his Englishry abroad with him and brings it home unchanged. Wherever he goes he consorts with other English tourists. By a good hotel he means one that is like an English hotel... In the same way a man may carry his modernity with him through all his reading of past literatures... the highlights for him are the bits that resemble – or can be so read that they seem to resemble – the poetry of his own age'. Far richer is the experience of the man who 'chooses to discover a foreign land, by meeting the people, eating the food, drinking the local wine,' and thus is able to 'see the foreign country as it looks, not to tourists, but to its inhabitants. So with old literature. You can go beyond the first impression that a poem makes on your modern sensibility'. The fourteenth century is probably as far from today's society as most readers will travel into that literary foreign country. It is a big step to make.

So we need some awareness of the significant events defining the Chaucerian world view. What shaped people's hopes and fears? What did they believe? How was society organised? These questions are considered in the first part of the book.

The language of the texts

The language used by Chaucer and other writers was startling and new. Enriched by vocabulary borrowed largely from French and Latin, it became the language of poetry, politics and state, steadily replacing French in civil courts, legal documents and historical records. In 1325 William of Nassyngton stated in his book *Mirror of Life:*

No Latyn wil I speke no waste
But English, that men use must
That can ech man understande
That is born in Ingelande.

I shall waste no time speaking Latin
but instead English, that men must use
that all men can understand
who were born in England.

Although wide variations in dialect existed across the country, it could be said by the end of the century that a Northumbrian could understand a Londoner (more or less) when both were using their 'mother tongue'. Standard English had arrived.

Chaucer considered in the context of other writers

For modern readers the works of Geoffrey Chaucer, and his *Canterbury Tales* in particular, dominate the English literature of this period. But he was not writing in isolation; nor do *The Canterbury Tales* define the manner in which he always wrote. This book looks at ways in which his texts reflect literary styles and conventions of his time, as well as ways in which he was influenced by other writers, alive and dead, English and foreign. Passages from contemporary works are included in Part 3 and throughout this book to compare with Chaucer's own, in content, style and quality. His position as the supreme writer of his time, the 'Father of English Literature', can thus be examined more critically. To Hoccleve and Lydgate, Chaucer's contemporaries, he was the 'first findere of our fayre langage', and 'floure of poets, thorghout al Bretayne'. His immediate influence is examined here, as well as his inspiration for later writers, who continue to assert their debt to and admiration of Chaucer's own works and the magnetism of the fascinating period we can call the age of Chaucer.

How this book is organised

Part 1: Approaching the Chaucerian age

An introduction to key issues: Chaucer's life and works; contemporary writers; the world Chaucer knew.

Part 2: Approaching the texts

An exploration of the language of the texts; the development of 'style' in English literature; literary influences on English writers; popular source material; the purpose of texts; how Chaucer's works relate to those of his contemporaries.

Part 3: Texts and extracts

A selection of texts and extracts from familiar and less well-known medieval scripts, some of which are referred to in other parts of the book, all of which may be used as a focus for tasks or assignments.

Part 4: Critical approaches

Responses to medieval literature in the past: its influence on later literature, art and architecture. Attempts to emulate and find affinity with the style and subject matter of Chaucer's age; current attitudes to medieval literature.

Part 5: Writing about Chaucer and other medieval texts

Responding to the language; recognising the author's aims; identifying the type of text; understanding literary conventions and how they are treated in any particular text; being aware of plot and characterisation within the genre; recognising differences between Chaucer's writing and that of his contemporaries; understanding influences affecting fourteenth century thought and literature.

Part 6: Resources

Guidance on further reading and useful websites; key dates; glossary of technical terms and index.

There are tasks and assignments throughout the text and at the end of Parts 1, 2, 4 and 5.

Wherever possible quotations from Chaucer's works have been taken from the Cambridge University Press, *Cambridge School Chaucer series* (published 1998 – 2001) or the earlier Cambridge University Press Chaucer series, edited by James Winny *et al*.

1 | **Approaching the Chaucerian age**

- What do you understand by the word 'medieval'? Where have your ideas of 'medievalism' come from? History? Literature (of the fourteenth century, or later)? Art?

- What are the main topics of writing of the fourteenth century that you have so far encountered?

- What fundamental aspects of life and attitudes have changed most since then?

- How relevant can such writings be for readers today?

Most readers first approach medieval literature through the opening lines of *The General Prologue* to Chaucer's *Canterbury Tales:*

> Whan that Aprill with his shoures soote
> The droghte of March hath perced to the roote,
> And bathed every veine in swich licour
> Of which vertu engendred is the flour;
> Whan Zephirus eek with his sweete breeth
> Inspired hath in every holt and heeth
> The tendre croppes, and the yonge sonne
> Hath in the Ram his halve cours yronne,
> And smale foweles maken melodie,
> That slepen al the night with open ye
> (So priketh hem nature in hir corages);
> Thanne longen folk to goon on pilgrimages,
> And palmeres for to seken straunge strondes,
> To ferne halwes, kowthe in sondry londes;
> And specially from every shires ende
> Of Engelond to Caunterbury they wende,
> The hooly blisful martir for to seke,
> That hem hath holpen whan that they were seeke.

The language is archaic, but the writer seems to be indulging in a recognisable English obsession with the weather. It's April, and it's raining. Only later does it become clear that rain on a dry land is a metaphor for spiritual awakening as much as a report on how the crops are growing.

But the next line or two of Chaucer's *General Prologue* refer to aspects of life that seem less familiar to us than April rain. Pilgrimages, holy martyrs, measuring of time and date by means of references to the signs of the zodiac – all suggest that much of what was an unremarkable part of life in the fourteenth century will require an effort of understanding by a modern reader. Chaucer and his contemporaries were writers of their time; insight into their works requires some awareness of their world.

Chaucer's life

Background

Geoffrey Chaucer's background, his circumstances and his varied lifestyle were all important in shaping the kind of writer he became. He was born to wealthy but not aristocratic parents. John and Agnes Chaucer lived comfortably in Thames Street, London, citizens of a city very different from today's in many ways, but then, as now, a place of sophistication and opportunity. The Chaucer family had moved from Ipswich in the early fourteenth century, and were well-established merchants in an environment where it was possible for a merchant's family to become 'gentry' within two or three generations, or even less.

The over-simplified division of society into three classes – aristocracy, clergy and peasants – had all but disappeared by the 1340s, and the possibility of improving one's social status was an important issue, and one that would frequently be the subject of Chaucer's personal life and his writings. The quality of *gentillesse* – truly gentlemanly or noble behaviour – was supposedly what distinguished nobly born people (whose families had owned land for centuries, bore coats of arms and held titles) from those who were merely 'churls', 'villeins' or peasants, with no social graces. In *The General Prologue* to *The Canterbury Tales* Chaucer gives a clear idea of the traditional behaviour and qualities of members of the aristocracy in descriptions of the Knight and his son, the Squire. A different view of *gentillesse* is given to one of his most disruptive and rebellious pilgrims, the Wife of Bath. During her tale, a low-born old woman gives this definition of true nobility to the knight she has tricked into marrying her:

> But, for ye speken of swich gentillesse
> As is descended out of old richesse,
> That therfore sholden ye be gentil men,
> Swich arrogance is nat worth an hen.
> Looke who that is moost vertuous alway,
> Privee and apert, and moost entendeth ay
> To do the gentil dedes that he kan;
> Taak him for the grettest gentil man.

Since you mention the sort of gentillesse
that is derived from a long line of wealthy ancestors,
and therefore this makes you 'gentlemen',
such presumption is useless [lit: not worth a hen].
Whoever behaves most virtuously at all times,
privately and publicly, and always tries hardest
to do all the virtuous actions he can,
take him as the example of the greatest 'gentleman'.

▶ Make a note of the various aspects of *gentillesse* apparent in the character studies of the Knight and the Squire from *The General Prologue* and in this quotation. What similarities and differences do you notice?

Education and early career

Young Geoffrey was carefully educated. He was literate, had some knowledge of Latin and more of French and was interested in arithmetic. His understanding of astronomy is apparent in several of his works, including the treatise he later wrote on the use of the astrolabe for navigation.

By the age of sixteen he was employed as a page in the household of the wife of Lionel, Edward III's son, later Duke of Clarence. Here he would have learnt the behaviour and skills required of a courtier. He probably met influential aristocrats, and would certainly have discovered the courtly romances popular amongst the nobility, which would figure largely in his own later writings. As a member of the Duke's household, he fought against the French in 1359, thus gaining experience of the hardships of war. Captured and imprisoned, he was released in early 1360, on payment of ransom money of £16, paid by Edward III himself. Clearly he was worth preserving; his subsequent career shows he was sent on a number of diplomatic missions to France, Spain, and Italy. He was involved in trade negotiations, peace treaties and marriage contracts – all areas which confirm the impression of the man gained from his writings, of someone both discreet and shrewdly observant, capable of judging character and with a good grasp of diplomacy.

Court connections

During the 1360s Chaucer became even more closely involved in the highest court circles; he married Philippa de Roet, daughter of a Flemish knight and maid-in-waiting to Queen Philippa, the Flemish wife of Edward III. Partly through his wife's family, Chaucer had strong links with John of Gaunt, the Duke of Lancaster, powerful and influential son of the king. If not a personal friend, Gaunt was certainly a generous patron of the poet. One of Chaucer's best known early poems, written around 1370, is *The Boke of the Duchess,* a lament for Blanche, the first

Duchess of Lancaster, who died in 1368. The young Chaucers were beginning to move in the most exclusive social circles, a privilege that would offer the poet discerning audiences for his literary efforts. His poetry was designed to be read aloud, for reading was a public entertainment then, and not all his listeners could read themselves.

▶ Choose a fairly short passage of Chaucer's writing with which you are familiar (any of his extracts from Part 3 could be used) and look closely at the style and tone. Are there indications that this was intended to be read aloud?

Foreign influences

Whilst in Italy, in the 1370s, Chaucer encountered the writings of Dante. His admiration for this acclaimed master of great poetry written in the vernacular (rather than the more usual Latin or French), gave Chaucer the impetus to attempt something similar in English. Like Dante, Chaucer developed a poetic style that appeared straightforward and simple, whilst containing sophisticated and subtle poetic construction. His debt to other great Italian writers, Boccaccio and Petrarch, is also obvious; he frequently used Italian settings and adaptations of their stories in his work.

Later years

There is little indication that Chaucer's life as a writer took precedence over his public image as a man of business. Certainly he was acclaimed as an entertaining and skilful poet at court, but he was also busy in political and financial circles at home and abroad. In 1374 he became Comptroller of Customs for the port of London, a position both lucrative and responsible. Later, as Clerk of the King's Works under Richard II, he dealt with the administration, construction and maintenance of royal buildings. Chaucer was appointed Knight of the Shire or parliamentary representative for Kent in 1386, suggesting that, like his creation the Franklin in *The Canterbury Tales,* he was a man of standing and wealth, although not a member of the nobility. At some time in the late 1380s he probably went on a pilgrimage. His final official position, as Deputy Warden of the forest of North Petherton, in his late 50s, was less demanding but still lucrative. He also continued to enjoy pensions derived from the royal and noble patronage he had regularly received. He may possibly have been an extravagant man; frequently he is recorded as asking for advances on the pension granted him by Richard II. After Richard's abdication, Chaucer wrote a *Lament to his Purse,* ruefully suggesting it was empty, and that the new king, Henry IV, might give him something to tide him over, by continuing the generous annuity he had been receiving from Richard:

To yow, my purse, and to noon other wight
Complayne I, for ye be my lady dere.
I am so sory, now that ye been lyght;
For certes but yf ye make me hevy chere,
Me were as leef be layd upon my bere;
For which unto your mercy thus I crye,
Beth hevy ageyn, or elles mot I dye.

To you, my purse, and to no other person
I address this complaint, for you are my dear lady.
I am so sorry you are light,
for truly, unless you take me seriously
I might as well be dead;
and so I beg for your mercy in this manner –
be heavy again, or else I must die.

▶ Chaucer is likening his purse to a mistress, who might be 'light' [promiscuous] or 'heavy' [seriously faithful]. From the tone of this extract, what can you discern of his position at court, and his rapport with the new king? (The annuity, incidentally, was duly paid.)

In 1400 Geoffrey Chaucer died in his newly-leased house in the gardens of Westminster Abbey. At the time of his death he was a retired civil servant, comfortably prosperous, and a highly acclaimed poet, celebrated by many contemporary admirers, whose influence and inspiration would endure to the present day. *The Canterbury Tales,* his last and most famous work, survives, incomplete.

In spite of the extraordinary amount of political upheaval during his lifetime, Chaucer seemed to avoid political controversy, however close he might be to the main protagonists. A clue to his ability for self-preservation may be found in the image of himself he presents in much of his work. Certainly no fool, he nevertheless deliberately adopted the role, as narrator, of wide-eyed naïvety in his accounts of his own behaviour and that of his fellow men and women. The picture of himself as a gullible and inoffensive member of the 'company' in *The Canterbury Tales* is a case in point, as are the two tales that 'Geoffrey Chaucer' the pilgrim, is given to tell. When the Miller tells a bawdy tale Chaucer disclaims any responsibility for it himself – he's only the narrator:

…whoso list it nat yheere,
Turne over the leef and chese another tale;
For he shal finde ynowe, grete and smale,
Of storial thing that toucheth gentillesse,
And eek moralitee and hoolinesse.

Blameth nat me if that ye chese amis.

...anyone who doesn't want to hear it
turn over and choose another tale;
he will find enough, both weighty and slighter
stories that are concerned with noble issues,
also moral and holy matters.
Don't blame me if you make the wrong choice.

His links with city merchants as well as members of the court meant that he never shunned the down-to-earth business of ordinary working life. His poetry is based upon observation of everyday people and things, as well as appreciation of the natural world. But his apparent modesty and unassuming stance did not disguise the fact that he was widely read in classical and contemporary works, and readily acknowledged his debt to other writers. His carefully constructed work is that of a man who practised his craft with skill, finesse and pride. Many critics consider *Troilus and Criseyde* to be his finest work; maybe Chaucer felt this too. His epilogue to this work is more than a conventional 'signing off' in the classic tradition; it combines artifice and simplicity, and allows the writer to place himself, humbly, among the greatest names in literature:

Go, litel bok, go, litel myn tragedye,
Ther God thi makere yet, er that he dye,
So sende myght to make in som comedye!
But litel book, no makyng thow n'envie,
But subgit be to alle poesye;
And kis the steppes where as thow seest pace
Virgile, Ovide, Omer, Lucan, and Stace.

Off you go, little book, be off, my little tragic story
And may God allow your author, before he dies,
to compose some comedy!
But, little book, do not be envious, or jealous,
but be subservient to all [great] poetry
and bend to kiss the steps where you see, passing by,
Virgil, Ovid, Homer, Lucan and Statius.

Chaucer's works

Chaucer never stopped writing; some pieces have been lost, but a brief account of his best known works gives an idea of his versatility. French literary influence is clear in his earliest works, for French was still the language of culture and romance in the fourteenth century, and many English writers chose to write in French or Latin; one of the most important things about Chaucer is that he chose to use English as the medium for poetry, and illustrated its diversity and richness. On the continent he was best known as a translator of works such as the *Roman de la Rose*, a thirteenth century French manuscript. He also translated from Latin the *Consolations* of the philosopher Boethius, a work enormously influential to his own way of thinking.

The Boke of the Duchess (1370?)

This is an elegy celebrating John of Gaunt's love for his wife Blanche; the poem's framework is a series of dreams, in one of which the dreamer meets a Black Knight, lamenting his dead 'Lady White'. The themes are love-sickness and the way in which such sickness works against the forces of nature. The idea of love as a sickness paralysing the lover, a hopeless yearning after an unattainable beloved, is central to the notion of 'courtly love' which dominated the French tradition. Here the narrator laments his lack of sleep, which is against the law of nature:

> And wel ye woot, agaynes kynde
> Hyt were to lyven in thys wyse,
> For nature wolde nat suffyse
> To noon erthly creature
> Nat longe tyme to endure
> Withoute slep and be in sorwe.

> *And you know well it is against the laws of nature*
> *to live in this way;*
> *Nature will not allow any living creature to exist for long*
> *without sleep, and in such misery.*

The House of Fame (1374/8?)

This was very probably written after Chaucer had encountered the works of Dante (he certainly travelled to Italy in 1373, the year in which the Florentine poet was honoured by his native city in a series of lectures given by Boccaccio). The poem is framed by a dream in which the narrator, guided by an eagle, explores various types of Fame: famous lovers, military heroes, kings, emperors and great poets. An illustration of the humorous English slant Chaucer gave to his Italian source material may be shown by the fact that, although Dante's poet narrator in the *Divina Commedia* is also guided by an eagle, it is only Chaucer's eagle that complains about the heaviness of his passenger (and there are several references to the poet's plumpness in his writings).

The Parlement of Fowles (1380?)

The subject of this poem is love, in all its guises – stated with clarity and artistry in the first lines (see page 45). This poem too is based around a dream in which the poet witnesses the 'parlement' of the title, at which birds, representing every status and degree of society in Chaucer's London world, debate the nature of love. The aristocrats of the fowl world favour courtly love whilst the lower classes, like the duck, pour scorn on this high-flown nonsense:

> 'Wel bourded,' quod the doke, 'by myn hat!
> That men shulde loven alwey causeles!
> Who can a resoun fynde or wit in that?'

> *'That's a funny joke!' said the duck,*
> *that men should always love without good cause!*
> *Where's the logic or sense in that?'*

Troilus and Criseyde (1381–6)

The poem tells a story originally derived from Homer's epic of the Trojan wars. Criseyde's father has defected to the Greeks leaving his daughter in Troy, in the care of her worldly uncle Pandarus. She and Troilus, son of the Trojan King Priam, fall in love. Eventually her father, Calchas, asks for his daughter to be returned to him, in exchange for a Trojan knight. Once in the Greek camp, in spite of all her promises of fidelity to Troilus, Criseyde surrenders to a smooth-talking Greek, Diomed.

Many see this as Chaucer's greatest poetic achievement – the work of a man secure in his reputation as a writer of the romance poetry most popular with his cultured audience. Although basing his poem on Boccaccio's *Il Filostrato* (The Lovesick Man), a contemporary rendering of the same source material, Chaucer adds richness and variety to his English version. His Criseyde (or Cressida) is treated with warm understanding; she is intelligent, quick-witted, resourceful; the reader responds to her with both sympathy and blame. The careful machinations of Pandarus add a comic dimension to the narrative. Courtly love is celebrated in Troilus' wooing, yet Chaucer invites his audience to realise such idealism is often at odds with life's realities. Fate intervenes, driving the lovers apart. The image of a man strapped helplessly to Fortune's wheel, which takes him to the heights then relentlessly plunges him into the depths, is a common symbol in medieval art. Quirks of Fate, which separate the lovers, destroying their relationship, are as important an aspect of the poem as the love which first draws them together. Chaucer pays tribute to the power of Fate or Fortune at moments of greatest happiness:

... O Fortune, executrice of wierdes,
O influences of thise hevenes hye!
Soth is, that under God ye ben oure hierdes,
Though to us bestes ben the causez wrie.

... Oh Fortune, dispenser of our fates,
and you too, controlling influence of the heavens above!
it is true, though less than God, you too are our shepherds
though the reasons for our destiny are hidden from us beasts.

The narrative is full of vivid images. Here is Criseyde's first sight of Troilus, returning triumphantly from battle:

His helm tohewen was in twenty places,
That by a tyssew heng his bak byhynde;
His sheeld todasshed was with swerdes and maces,
In which men myghte many an arwe fynde
That thirled hadde horn and nerf and rynde;
And ay the peple cryde, 'Here cometh oure joye,
And, nexte his brother, holder up of Troye!'

For which he wex a litel reed for shame
When he the peple upon hym herde cryen,
That to byholde it was a noble game
How sobrelich he caste down his yen.
Criseyda gan al his chere aspien,
And leet so softe in hire herte synke,
That to hireself she seyde, 'Who yaf me drynke?'

His helmet was ripped in twenty places
and hung behind him by a thread;
his shield was battered by swords and maces
and men could see the signs that arrows
had pierced the horn, skin and gut
and the people kept crying 'Here comes our hero,
alongside his brother [Hector] *Troy's saviour!'*

And so he blushed a little with embarrassment
when he heard them call out about him.
It was a rare noble treat to see him:
how humbly he looked down.
Cressida saw his demeanour
and allowed it to sink deep into her heart

so that she said to herself 'What have I been
given to drink?' [i.e. some love-potion]

The Canterbury Tales (1387–1400)

More detailed discussion of this work occurs in Part 2. Chaucer worked on the *Tales*
during the last ten years or so of his life. He used the formula, popular at the time,
of a collection of stories held together by a specific framework, a device most
notably used by Boccaccio (see page 66). Chaucer introduces a group of pilgrims
who represent a wide spectrum of society. This allows him to offer very varied
stories and styles of story-telling, all told by characters over whom Chaucer says he
has no control, since he merely reports what others say.

▶ Chaucer disclaims all responsibility for the words and actions of others in *The
Canterbury Tales*. What does this suggest about the author himself, his characters
and the audience the author addresses? Look at the following excerpt from his
description of the Monk: Chaucer may seem impartial – but is he really
manipulating our response in this passage?

This ilke Monk leet olde thinges pace,
And heeld after the newe world the space.
He yaf nat of that text a pulled hen,
That seith that hunters ben nat hooly men,
Ne that a monk, whan he is recchelees,
Is likned til a fissh that is waterlees, —
This is to seyn, a monk out of his cloistre.
But thilke text heeld he nat worth an oystre;
And I seyde his opinion was good.
What sholde he studie and make himselven wood,
Upon a book in cloistre alwey to poure?

This Monk here let old things pass him by,
and eagerly followed new trends.
He didn't give a plucked hen for the religious rule
that says hunters are not godly men,
nor that a monk, when dismissive of his monastic vows
is like a fish out of water,
in other words, a monk out of his cloister.
He said such rules weren't worth an oyster [very cheap then]
And I agreed with his opinion.
Why should he send himself mad with studying,
always poring over a book in the cloisters?

Many different types of people went on pilgrimages, and for various reasons. The tales are offered up for comparison with one another by the addition of a 'story-telling competition' organised by the Host of the Tabard Inn. The stated intention (uncompleted) was that each pilgrim should tell two stories on the outward journey and two on the way back; these stories often reflect their different interests and status in society. All stories are then held up for praise, criticism or ridicule by their fellow travellers and, of course, by the author's wider audience.

Over thirty characters are included in Chaucer's group of pilgrims, if you include all five guildsmen, the priest and nuns who accompany the Prioress, and the Canon's Yeoman, who arrives *en route*. His full plan was never realised. The group never reaches Canterbury, and, apart from Chaucer himself, no pilgrim tells more than one tale. Some stories had probably been written much earlier, and were adapted by the author to fit his scheme (*The Knight's Tale* is one of these). Many derived from other stories already well known to the fourteenth century audience.

The order in which the stories were originally intended to appear has been the subject of considerable debate (and maybe Chaucer himself had not finally decided). Some tales seem to have lost their prologues or epilogues; others were plainly intended for a specific narrator, whilst a few seem to have little kinship with the pilgrims to whom they have been designated.

All the tales were intended to promote discussion and debate; no single tale offers a definitive moral standpoint. Chaucer presents characters with attitudes and beliefs different from his own, and rarely offers an authorial judgement. His original audience would have approached the reading of the tales prepared to take an active part in discussing and questioning all aspects of the text. Modern readers need to be prepared to do likewise.

▶ Read the following section from the Prologue to *The Pardoner's Tale,* in which the Pardoner explains how he makes his living. How successfully might such a passage provoke discussion in an audience?

> I stonde lyk a clerk in my pulpet,
> And whan the lewed peple is doun yset,
> I preche so as ye han herd bifoore,
> And telle an hundred false japes moore.
> Thanne peyne I me to strecche forth the nekke,
> And est and west upon the peple I bekke,
> As dooth a dowve sittinge on a berne.
> Mine handes and my tonge goon so yerne
> That it is joye to se my bisynesse.
> Of avarice and of swich cursednesse
> Is al my preching, for to mak hem free

To yeven hir pens, and namely unto me.
For myn entente is nat but for to winne,
And nothing for correccioun of sinne.

I stand like a cleric in the pulpit,
and when the simple folk have sat down
I preach as I have already explained to you,
and tell a hundred more fine false tales.
I take pains to stretch forward my neck
bending down towards the people, east and westwards,
just like a dove on a barn roof.
So eagerly do I ply my hands and tongue
it's a delight to see me at my trade.
I preach about greed, and similar accursed things,
to persuade them to be generous
in giving their pennies – particularly giving them to me.
For my only motive is gain.
I care nothing about correcting sinfulness.

Chaucer's contemporaries

Although perhaps the most famous writer of his age, Chaucer was not writing in an artistic vacuum. Under Richard II in particular, the royal court offered patronage to writers, artists and musicians. Some preferred to write in French or Latin, but men (and women) increasingly chose to write prose, poetry and drama in English. Important works were presented in English, by people such as John Trevisa, a Gloucestershire priest who translated two important texts on history and natural history from Latin. Popular lyrics and works by anonymous writers in English also survive from this time, as well as better known manuscripts. Some wrote for London sophisticates, others for down-to-earth inhabitants of York or Coventry. Very often authors echo themes found in Chaucer's works, and frequently use similar sources for their tales, though tone and style may differ from his.

The *Gawain* poet

The story of Sir Gawain and the Green Knight appeared in a manuscript of around 1390. The poet's identity remains a mystery, though the dialect in which it is written suggests he came from the north-west. It is a complex tale told with sophistication. Sir Gawain, one of King Arthur's knights, accepts a challenge from the Green Knight as a test of physical bravery, but finds his real test takes place in the bedchamber, withstanding the seductive wiles of his host's wife. Like Chaucer, the poet examines romantic ideals, and asks how convincingly such behaviour can cope with the actualities of the real world. It is a tale that combines the world of magic (the decapitated Green Knight miraculously rides off carrying his head) with a vivid realisation of the natural world, the thrills and violence of the hunt and the comfortable luxury of life in a wealthy household. It is a poem full of irony and humour, as for example in this passage in which Sir Gawain, snuggling up in bed whilst his host is out hunting, realises, with some perplexity, that his beautiful hostess has secretly joined him:

> And as in slomeryng he slode, sleyly he herde
> A litel dyn at his dor, and derfly open;
> And he heves up his hed out of the clothes,
> A corner of the cortyn he caght up a lyttel,
> And waytes warly thiderwarde quat hit be myght.
> Hit was the ladi, loflyest to beholde,
> That drow the dor after hir ful dernly and stylle,
> And bowed towarde the bed; and the burne schamed
> And layde hym doun lystyly and let as he slepte.
> And ho stepped stilly and stel to his bedde,
> Kest up the cortyn and creped withinne,
> And set hir ful softly on the bed-syde
> And lenged there selly longe, to loke quen he wakened.

> *And, lying half asleep, he heard a stealthy sound,*
> *a little noise at his door, which opened speedily;*
> *And he lifts his head out of the bedclothes*
> *lifts up a corner of the bedcurtain*
> *and peers warily out to see what it might be.*
> *It was the lady, loveliest to behold,*
> *who shut the door behind her with care and silently*
> *and moved to the bed; and the bashful man*
> *lay there quietly and pretended he was asleep.*
> *She stepped silently and stealthily to the bed,*
> *lifted the hangings and slipped inside*
> *and sat gently on the edge of the bed*
> *and waited a considerable length of time for him to wake up.*

The northern pronunciation is apparent in the use of 'qu' in words such as 'what' and 'when' – producing a sound still heard in Scots pronunciation today.

▶ What comparisons can you make between this passage and Chaucer's description of two young knights from *The Knight's Tale* on page 83 in both style and content? (Consider the humour, and the behaviour of the knight and the lady.)

William Langland

Langland's final version of *The Vision of Piers Plowman* probably dates from 1380. Like many of Chaucer's earlier works, it employs the device of dreams to deal with its themes. Unlike Chaucer, Langland directly confronts social problems. He sees a greedy and corrupt society, seemingly unaware of important spiritual concerns. In a series of dreams the narrator encounters Piers Plowman, symbol of the simple, straightforward Christian man, who inspires and leads him on a pilgrimage to find Truth. The poem highlights the lack of leadership or inspiration offered by the established church and develops into a study of the need for self-examination in each individual's search for spiritual truth. Emphasis on the importance of the individual in society (as opposed to generalised social categories – knights, churchmen, labourers) was an important development in fourteenth century literature. In a debate with Reason and Conscience the narrator, Will, talks of his worldly life, time wasted in pursuit of wealth and property. Nevertheless he lives in the optimistic belief that somehow his sins will be forgiven at his death, hoping that speedy repentance then will earn him a place in heaven. He is given the clear warning that soul-searching and penitence cannot be left so late:

> 'So hope I to have of hym that is almyghty
> A gobet of his grace, and bigynne a tyme
> That alle tymes of my tyme to profit shal turne.'
> 'I rede the,' quod Resoun tho, 'rape the to bigynne
> The lyf that is louable and leele to thy soule' –
> 'Ye, and contynue!'quod Conscience; and to the kyrke I wente.

> *So I hope to have from almighty God*
> *a morsel of his grace, so that a period will begin*
> *that will turn my whole lifespan to eternal profit.*
> *But Reason said, 'I advise you to hurry to start*
> *a good life, both admirable and worthy for your soul'.*
> *Yes, and persevere with it,' said Conscience; and I proceeded to the*
> *church.*

▶ What does Langland's more critical tone suggest about the audience for which he writes?

John Gower

Gower, London man of property, wealthy, with a legal background, moved in similar circles to Chaucer. He and Chaucer were friends and influenced each other's work. Gower wrote much of his poetry in French and Latin; it was probably Chaucer's influence that persuaded him to use English for his greatest work, the

Confessio Amantis, written around the same time as Chaucer was writing *The Canterbury Tales.*

    Confessio Amantis is a collection of stories about love in all its guises. Gower's framework for the tales is a dialogue between Amans, the lover, and his instructor in the 'religion of love', a priest of Venus. The sins of love are categorised according to the seven deadly sins of the Bible, and seem to correspond in some way with the faults in society as a whole. Gower was a more politically motivated writer than Chaucer; his early work, in French, *Mirour de l'Omme,* was a satirical analysis of contemporary social categories, from which Chaucer borrowed freely in his *General Prologue.* Just as Chaucer used many of *The Canterbury Tales* to make implicit comment about people's inability to live up to ideals of behaviour, similarly Gower points out, in the passage below, how far the behaviour of the knight, Tereus, has fallen below standards of chivalry. Having raped his sister-in-law, Philomene, he tears out her tongue, so she cannot tell of his behaviour:

> And he thanne as a lyon wod
> With hise unhappi handes stronge
> Hire cauhte be the tresses longe,
> With whiche he bond ther bothe hire armes –
> That was a fieble dede of armes! –
> And to the grounde anon hire caste
> And out he clippeth also faste
> Hire tunge with a peire scheres.

> *And then, like a mad lion*
> *with his dreadfully powerful hands*
> *he grabbed her by her long hair,*
> *using it to bind both her arms –*
> *what a wretched feat of arms that was! –*
> *and threw her straight away down on the ground,*
> *and as fast as he could he cut out*
> *her tongue with a pair of shears.*

▶ What similarities can you notice between Gower's vocabulary and Chaucer's?

Thomas Hoccleve

Hoccleve (1368–1426) was a Londoner, and a poet all his life. Like Chaucer, he translated works from French and wrote works intended for a courtly audience. He admired and imitated Chaucer's verse, and adopted a ruefully humorous tone similar to Chaucer's own, particularly here in his account of *La Male Regle,* or the 'badly mismanaged' life, of T. Hoccleve:

Wher was a gretter maister eek than I,
Or bet aqweyntid at Westmynstre Yate?
Among the taverneres namely
And cookes whan I cam eerly or late,
I pynchid nat at hem in myn acate
But paied hem as that they axe wolde;
Wherfore I was the welcomere algate
And for a verray gentil man yholde.

And where was there a better man than myself
or more well-known at Westminster Gate?
Especially among the pub landlords
or cooks, at the beginning or end of the working day.
I never queried the amount of my bill
but paid them what they asked;
and so I was always most welcome
and reckoned to be a real gentleman.

John Wyclif

Works like those of Gower and Chaucer were intended primarily to entertain. The Bible, translated by the scholar John Wyclif during the last twenty years of the fourteenth century, was written to give ordinary people access to the primary source of their Christian religion. Until this work was produced all Biblical knowledge had been filtered through the interpretation of priests, since only they could read and understand the Latin version used in church. Wyclif's translation was as straightforward and literal as could be achieved.

Mystical writings

Great interest in individual soul-searching played an important part in the spiritual life of many people, at a time when there was increasing emphasis on taking responsibility for one's own spiritual health rather than leaving it to the established church.

The Cloud of Unknowing – possibly written by a priest towards the end of the century – discusses how to achieve closeness to God through contemplation. By rejecting earthly ties and accepting the impenetrable mystery of spiritual matters, one could attain the state of joyful unknowing worship that the writer proposes:

...of God himself can no man thinke. And therfore I wol leve *[I shall turn away from]* al that thing that I can think, *[that I can imagine and understand]* and chese to my love *[and choose to adore]* that thing that I cannot think, for-whi *[for this reason]* he may wel be loved, bot not thought. By love may he be getyn and holden, bot bi thought neither. *[We may gain awareness of God through loving him, but will never do so through intellectual pursuit of what he is.]*

Julian of Norwich was a mystic, born in 1342, who lived as a hermit, or anchoress, in Norwich, devoting her life to prayer. Her visions, experienced in 1373 and recorded in her revelations around 1390, made her renowned as a spiritual guide. Her writings focused on Christ's crucifixion; the style is simple, but more personal and passionate than that used by the previous writer:

> ... sodenly I saw the reed bloud rynnyng downe from under the garlande, hote and freyshely, plentuously and lively, right as it was in the tyme that the garland of thornes was pressed on his blessed hede. Right so, both God and man, the same that sufferd for me, I conceived truly and mightly that it was himselfe that shewed it me without anie mene *[intermediary]*.
> And in the same shewing sodeinly the trinitie fulfilled my hert most of joy, and so I understode it shall be in heven without end to all that shall come ther.

Many were moved and inspired by her determination to reach full understanding of her God and her religion; among them Margery Kempe, whose book of visions and spiritual outpourings was not written down until the 1430s, but who was a well-known visionary and outspoken mystic of the late fourteenth century.

Chaucer's Parson shows a similar concern for spiritual awareness beyond everyday concerns. Presented in *The General Prologue* as the ideal churchman, his importance in the pattern of the complete *Canterbury Tales* can be seen by the positioning of his tale as well as its content. His is the last contribution by a pilgrim. The Parson uses no tale or parable to illustrate his theme. His carefully constructed sermon on the nature of repentance reminds his audience of man's need for sincere preparation before reaching life's ultimate destination. Even the master of ceremonies and landlord of the Tabard, Harry Bailly, recognises the need to set one's spiritual house in order:

> 'Telleth,' quod he, 'youre meditacioun.
> But hasteth yow; the sonne wole adoun;
> Beth fructuous, and that in litel space.
> And to do wel God sende yow his grace.'

> *Tell us your deliberations*
> *but hurry, the sun is nearly set;*

be constructive and also be brief
and may God give you grace [in your efforts to save us].

York Mystery Plays

Performed by various craft guilds or 'mysteries', these religious plays effectively relayed Bible stories to common people in an entertaining, colourful way. Many were still presented in anglicised French even as late as the fourteenth century, but the York plays survive in their original English. They date from the time just after the Black Death of 1348, when York was the flourishing and wealthy capital of the north. They made Biblical tales relevant to everyday life, in verse often unrefined and robust.

▶ What does the passage from the Old Testament story of the Flood on page 94 in Part 3 suggest about the traditional roles of ordinary men and women in both religious matters and everyday life?

John Mandeville

Mandeville's *Travels* (c.1390–1400) is the first popular travel guide in English. This collection of information and fable offered exciting facts about the world beyond Europe. Much accurate data about the Holy Land and northern Africa is given, but the second part of the book contains some splendid fantasy, described so plausibly that Mandeville's *Travels* were to remain one of the most popular books of the fifteenth and sixteenth centuries. Columbus took a copy with him when he set sail in 1492. Mandeville's useful account of Jerusalem is on page 29 of this book. Here is his description of the people who inhabit a more distant country:

> ... And in another yle also ben folk that han non hedes *[have no heads]*, and here eyen and here mouth ben behynde in here schuldres *[their eyes and mouths are behind their shoulders]*. And in another yle ben folk that han the face all platt *[completely flat]*, all pleyn withouten nese and withouten mouth *[without nose or mouth]*. But thei han ii. smale holes all rounde instede of hire eyen, and hire mouth is platt also withouten lippes. And in another yle ben folk of foul fasceoun and schapp *[dreadful shape and form]* that han the lippe above the mouth so gret that whan thei slepen in the sonne thei keveren all the face with that lippe *[when they sleep in the sun they cover the whole face with that lip]*. And in another yle ...'

A similar mixture of truth and exotic fable is used by Shakespeare in his account of Othello's travels, when the hero speaks of:

> ... antres vast and deserts idle,
> Rough quarries, rocks and hills whose heads touch heaven,
> It was my hint to speak, such was the process;
> and of the Cannibals that each other eat,
> The anthropophagi, and men whose heads
> Do grow beneath their shoulders.

► It is unlikely that Mandeville's original audience believed all his tales, any more than Shakespeare's listeners believed in the anthropophagi. Why did audiences enjoy hearing about monstrous creatures that were probably non-existent? Is this still the case?

The world Chaucer knew

Town and country

London was England's largest city by far; yet it contained fewer than 90,000 people, a population that was to shrink further after the Black Death of 1348, when between one third and a half of the population of England died. So small was the city, that the sound of Bow bells (St. Mary's Arches) – rung in the evenings to signal the closing of the city gates – could be heard by anyone still working in the surrounding fields. And yet it was the largest centre of population in the country, only York and Bristol coming anywhere near it in size and status. It was a bustling and lively place. The Cook who travels with the Canterbury pilgrims comes from London. His unfinished tale about a lively apprentice captures the pleasure-loving vitality of a typical London youth:

> At every bridale wolde he singe and hoppe;
> He loved bet the taverne than the shoppe.
> For whan ther any riding was in Chepe,
> Out of the shoppe thider wolde he lepe –
> Til that he hadde al the sighte yseyn,
> And daunced wel, he wolde nat come ayeyn –
> And gadered him a meynee of his sort
> To hoppe and singe and maken swich disport;

> *He would dance and caper at every wedding;*
> *He preferred the pub to the shop.*
> *For if anything went on in Cheapside [busy shopping street]*
> *Off there he'd go, out of the shop*
> *until he had seen all that was going on*
> *and enjoyed a dance, and he wouldn't come back*
> *but collected a gang of like-minded mates*
> *to dance and sing and enjoy themselves.*

Only five per cent of the population lived in communities large enough to be called towns. Most lived in villages, often sited near a manor house or monastery; by far the greatest part of the population was involved in agriculture. Vast areas of countryside were covered by forest and woodland – prime hunting land, such as Chaucer's Monk, the 'prikasour' with his greyhounds and fine horse, would have relished. Roads were unpaved, and often impassable in winter months. Travelling without company could be lonely and dangerous; *The Friar's Tale* is an account of a Summoner who meets the Devil himself 'under a forest syde'. Forest land was fiercely protected by hunting rights, and only a few solitary woodsmen or outlaws lived there. Tales of Robin Hood can be traced to the fourteenth century: in a ballad written within eighty years of Chaucer's death, a nervous monk is offered company on his journey through the forest with these words:

> ... Robyn Hode has many a wilde felow,
> I tell you in certeyn;
> If thei wist ye rode this way,
> In feith ye shulde be slayn.

> *Robin Hood has many wild companions,*
> *I tell you for sure*
> *If they knew you were riding along here,*
> *truly, you would be killed.*

No wonder Chaucer's pilgrims agreed to form a group to make the two and a half day's journey from London to Canterbury. No wonder the journey through forest and wild north-western countryside in *Sir Gawain and the Green Knight* attains such significance in the poem, a journey of such hardship that the freezing rain, sleet and rocky heights seem far more terrible than any enemy the knight might encounter.

Travel at home

Although a large percentage of the population, particularly in rural areas, rarely travelled more than twenty miles from their birthplace, it would be a mistake to assume that there was little journeying from one place to another. Chaucer's pilgrims used a well-trodden path when they set off from London to Canterbury. All manner of people came to London: cramped, noisy and busy, it was the commercial and political heart of England, attracting the ambitious from all parts of the country. Chaucer's own family came from the Ipswich area. Scholars from Oxford and Cambridge often had business in London.

In his Prologue to *Piers Plowman* William Langland writes of the many priests who travelled to London to earn a living as chantry priests (saying prayers for the dead) after the Black Death had severely reduced their income from their depleted parishes:

> Persones and parsche prestis pleyned to the bischop
> That here parsches were pore sithe this pestelence tyme,
> To have a licence and a leve in Londoun to dwelle
> And synge ther for symonye while selver is so swete.

> *Parsons and parish priests begged the bishop,*
> *for their parishes were poor since the plague,*
> *to have licence and permit to live in London*
> *singing prayers for payment, for silver is so sweet.*

This must have been quite commonplace; Chaucer mentions it too, in *The General Prologue* to *The Canterbury Tales,* contrasting his own portrait of the conscientious poor Parson with those who:

> ran to Londoun unto Seinte Poules
> To seken him a chaunterie for soules,
> Or with a bretherhed *[trade guild]* to been witholde;

In fact, *The General Prologue* shows quite clearly how London lured an enormous variety of people.

Other travellers included itinerant friars, Dominican and Franciscan, who travelled extensively, preaching in towns and villages along the way – a method of communication later to be used by Wyclif's followers, the Lollards. Groups of travelling players, pedlars, messengers and pilgrims were on the move from the first days of spring until the sleet and snow of winter made all but the most essential of journeys a wretched experience. For life was dominated by the passing of days and seasons in a way not easy to grasp in an age when central heating and artificial lighting makes us less aware of nature. The first mechanical clocks were only just beginning to appear in rich households during the 1340s. Most people reckoned time according to daylight hours, and the movements of sun, moon and stars. The medieval year began in March, with the first stirrings of life in fields and woods, a time that also heralded for every man a reconsideration of his spiritual condition. A pilgrimage was certainly a 'holy-day' – an opportunity to review past happenings and actions unencumbered by the normal ties of everyday life – but it was also a holiday, and some of Chaucer's pilgrims have this aspect of their journey very firmly in mind.

▶ Read the first eighteen lines of *The General Prologue,* printed on page 8, and consider how Chaucer suggests people are stirred by both instincts and spiritual motives in springtime.

Foreign travel

In the centuries following the Norman conquest many landowners owned property on both sides of the English Channel and travelled between their estates. At the height of the crusading era, during the twelfth and thirteenth centuries, knights with their retinues travelled even further afield. The Knight in Chaucer's *General Prologue* apparently saw service in many parts of Europe, Egypt, Russia and Turkey, and although it would have been difficult for one man to see action in so many places, he represents a group of people who fought in every corner of Christendom and 'hethenesse'. Increasingly, friars journeyed backwards and forwards to Rome, collecting the pardons they then sold to those needing forgiveness for sins. Merchants, particularly those involved in the wool trade, did most of their business with buyers in the Low Countries. All brought back to the quiet country parishes news of a fast-changing world.

Pilgrimages were popular, and the pilgrimage routes to the most popular shrines in the Holy Land and at Santiago de Compostella in Spain became busy tourist trails. A line of hostels across France into Spain was controlled by the great abbey at Cluny; travellers' guides were produced giving details of what to look for in the cathedral of St. James in Santiago; regular ferry services crossed the Mediterranean to the Holy Lands; Mandeville's *Travels* offered full accounts of the unmissable sights in Jerusalem:

> Also fro Jerusalem toward the west is a fair chirche where the tree of the cros grew. And ii. myle fro thens is a faire chirche where oure Lady mette with Elizabeth whan thei weren bothe with childe, and Seynt John stered in his modres wombe [*stirred in his mother's womb*] and made reverence to his creatour that he saugh not. And under the awtier [*altar*] of that chirche is the place where Seynt John was born. And fro that chirche is a myle to the castelle of Emaux, and there also oure Lord schewed him to ii. of his disciples after his resurrexioun. ... Also fro Jerusalem ii. myle is the Mount Joye, a fulle fair place and a delicyous, and there lyth Samuel the prophete in a fair tombe. And men clepen it [*call it*] Mount Joye for it yeveth [*gives*] joye to pilgrymes hertes because that there men seen first [*get their first sight of*] Jerusalem.

The changing shape of society

In *Piers Plowman,* William Langland displayed enormous concern about the breakdown of the 'old order'. At one point Piers pledges his service to a knight, reminding him, and all readers, of the stability and order life should possess:

> I shal swynke and swete and sowe for us bothe
> And labory for tho thou lovest al my lyf-tyme.
> In covenant that thou kepe holy Kerke and mysuelve
> Fro wastores and fro wikked men that this world struyen,

> *I shall work and sweat and sow corn for us both,*
> *and labour, too, for your love, all my life*
> *by the pact that you keep Holy Church and myself*
> *from wastrels and evil men who ruin the world;*

But Piers was looking back to a time already vanishing, if it ever existed. Even the least significant members of society – the labourers, tied to the land and their masters – became increasingly aware of the world beyond the fields they worked. In the earlier medieval period of the eleventh and twelfth centuries the traditional view had divided society into 'three estates': the gentry – knights of every degree of wealth and status, whose role was to rule, control and protect society; the church – men (and women) who would pray for the souls of all, and who thus bore responsibility for the spiritual life of the state; and the peasants – who worked the fields, served in the houses, and tended to the bodily needs of their superiors. This idealised view of a 'world order' in which all knew their places and roles in society, and accepted them, would never be fully achievable. By the end of the fourteenth century some men who had been born peasants were owning land, employing servants, even sending their sons to university, and aspiring towards the lifestyle and attitudes of their erstwhile masters. And women, traditionally the 'second sex' with little apparent say in public affairs, were often asserting their status in many ways. Events of the fourteenth century did much to speed up social and economic changes.

▶ Look at the list of characters described in *The General Prologue*. How easy is it to divide them according to the definitions of the 'three estates'?

The war with France

War between France and England lasted from 1337 until 1453, and resulted in a number of changes in English society, including a new 'nationalistic' fervour, favouring English as the language of state and literature. It also drained the resources of the crown (and therefore increased taxation of the people) and offered opportunities for foreign travel among the less wealthy. The English army needed armourers, grooms, cooks, wheelwrights, blacksmiths; and, since men were recruited from all parts of England, some members of the peasant classes began (often for the first time) to see something of life beyond their own villages. The army included not only knights on horseback – the traditional fighting machines of the early middle ages – but trained bowmen, usually from rural working backgrounds. Just as the Great War of 1914 disrupted the settled life of post-Victorian England, so men and women of the fourteenth century found themselves, willingly or not, grasping ideas and attitudes from other cultures. They also discovered, as every age discovers to its cost, that fighting is not glamorous, exciting or heroic. However much it might be glorified in art or literature, war was brutish, savage and ugly.

Chaucer understood both the glory and the horror of war. Compare, for example this description of the Temple of Mars, from *The Knight's Tale,* with the account of the exploits of the Knight himself from *The General Prologue:*

Ther saugh I first the derke imagining
Of Felonye, and al the compassing;
The crueel Ire, reed as any gleede;
The pykepurs, and eek the pale Drede;
The smilere with the knyf under the cloke;
The shepne brenninge with the blake smoke;
The tresoun of the mordringe in the bedde;
The open werre, with woundes al bibledde;
Contek, with blody knyf and sharp manace.
Al ful of chirking was that sory place.

There I first saw the dark images
Of Vice and all its aspects;
cruel Wrath, red as any glowing coal;
the petty thief and also pale Fear;
the smiler, with the knife beneath his cloak;
the barn burning with black smoke;
the outrage of murdering those asleep;
the open warfare with blood-spattered wounded;
battle, with bloody knife and fierce menace.
That dreadful place was full of harsh sounds.

Previously battles were dominated by cavalry charges of knights on huge war horses or *destriers.* Knights believed the support given by crossbowmen and foot soldiers was marginal, and that fortunes of war depended on their skill as trained, powerful, armoured, mounted men. Once overcome, opponents usually surrendered, in return for the ransom traditional codes of honour required (no point, of course, in sparing the lives of unprofitable peasant foot soldiers). Rituals of war were elaborate; young nobles trained in horsemanship and use of lance, sword and mace, testing their skills in jousts and tournaments. Battles could be decided by single combat between two opposing champions: Chaucer's Knight had fought in the lists three times 'and ay slayn his foo'. Undoubtedly the knight was a fearsome fighting machine; a contemporary ballad calls him 'a terrible worm in an iron cocoon'. And he was inevitably of noble birth, a bearer of arms and, in many cases, quite justifiably admired as one who dedicated his life to protecting his lord and his country. The contempt felt by many knights for foot soldiers as ineffectual and largely unreliable was partly understandable. Even crossbowmen usually failed to inflict much damage in the face of determined cavalry charges.

But during the wars against the Scots in the 1330s the English longbowmen (faster and more accurate than crossbowmen) had demonstrated their effectiveness against cavalry. At the battle of Crécy, 1346, faced with overwhelming French opposition, Edward III defied tradition by placing them in the vanguard. The bowmen successfully shattered the initial charge uphill by reckless French knights, and then themselves attacked in a downhill surge. By midnight over 4000 French knights lay dead. The status of the longbowman was assured by 1363, when the king decreed that the Sunday afternoon leisure activity for working men should be archery practice instead of football.

The professional soldier – and the erosion of 'chivalry'

As the century progressed, war between France and England, and disputes between supporters of two rivals for the papacy, led to some of the dirtiest fighting of the time, tarnishing the old image of the 'verray parfit gentil knyght'. Examples of knighthood at its best could still be found during the Hundred Years' War, in such figureheads as the Black Prince and Sir John Chandos. Froissart immortalised Chandos in his *Chronicles* as possessor of all the essential qualities of prowess, loyalty, courtesy and restraint. When he died in a skirmish in the 1370s, reports tell of his men weeping for their 'sage and ymaginatif' leader, wringing their hands and tearing their hair, crying out 'Ah, Sir John Chandos, flowre of chivalry, unhappily was forged the glaive *[blade]* that thus hath wounded you!'

But the new professional soldiers were ambitious, pitiless mercenaries, like Sir John Hawkwood. Knights had always fought for profit, as well as honour, but he and many others appeared more grasping and less honourable. Originally a poor knight in the English army of the 1350s, Hawkwood made his fortune by hiring himself and his troop of 5000 disciplined fighters, known from their distinctive tunics and brightly polished armour as the White Company, to the highest bidder. Frequently changing his allegiance, his only reservation was a refusal to fight against the English king. After a successful career of murder and destruction he died in Florence, respected and rich, Captain of the city state. The age of chivalry was becoming merely a memory, albeit an important one; but the ideal of the chivalrous, 'gentil' knight was still a powerful literary convention, as well as a reminder of the superior standards that nobles claimed as their birthright.

The Black Death

A catastrophe far more terrible even than war was to sweep through Europe, accelerating the social and economic changes in every part of the continent. Froissart, writing in the 1360s, reported that 'a third of the world has died'. The Black Death reached England in 1348, to return in 1361 and 1368, creating economic chaos, social unrest, high prices, profiteering, depravity and social and religious hysteria. Because the source of the plague was unknown, people saw it as a visitation from God, his punishment on a cursed and irreligious society. Whole communities were wiped out. In a remote part of Ireland one monk was left among his dead companions, to record their passing. He wrote 'I leave parchment to continue the work, if perchance any man survive and any of the race of Adam escape this pestilence and carry on the work which I have done'. He died, but his words outlived him. Ordinary people saw whole families, whole villages dying, and some looked in vain to their local clergy for comfort, finding it instead in the upsurge of interest in mysticism. It was reported that more commoners died than wealthy people – presumably because they had closer contact with the black rats and their fleas that carried the deadly virus. Those who could afford to, left the confines of cities and escaped to country retreats, like Boccaccio's lords and ladies in the *Decameron*. Tens of thousands of the valuable sheep, whose wool was such an essential part of the English economy, lay bloated and dying in the fields of East Anglia, reported the chronicler Knighton.

► How would you expect such widespread devastation to affect the views of society, as expressed in the art and literature of the time?

Although the aftermath of the Black Death brought a period of deprivation and hardship, for many it was also a time of great opportunity. Every branch of society lost some of its skilled workforce. Winchester Cathedral, for example, was being rebuilt in the 1340s, when the elaborate, complex handcarving produced in the era before the Black Death came to a sudden halt for twenty-five years; so many of the trained sculptors, carvers and other craftsmen died, that when work resumed in the 1370s the style was noticeably less elaborate, less demanding. All the same, those who survived found their services urgently needed.

A new breed of 'gentlemen'

Traditionally destined to work their lords' lands as generations of their forebears had done, the depleted population that took stock of itself in the aftermath of the Black Death quickly came to realise that the agricultural labour they provided was at a premium. In *Piers Plowman* William Langland describes the wage labourers who demand high wages and decent food for their services:

> Laborers that han no lond to lyve on but here handes
> Deynede noght to dyne a-day of nyhte-olde wortes;
> May no peny-ale hem pay ne no pece of bacoun
> But hit be fresh flesch or fisch, yfried or ybake,

> *Landless workers, who live off their own handiwork,*
> *refused to eat stale leftovers,*
> *would take no pay in weak ale or bacon bits,*
> *demanded fresh meat or fish, fried or baked.*

Enterprising commoners began acquiring lands and employing their own workforce, until over the course of one or two generations some might even own estates as large as those of the lesser aristocracy. Such wealthy landowners, not ennobled, but certainly not serfs or labourers, were called franklins, a word that originally meant 'free men'.

Perhaps because of a desperate need for money to finance his wars with France, Edward III had already begun to bestow knighthoods on wealthy London merchants: John Pulteney, draper, in 1337, and later Richard de la Pole, and the fishmongers, Robert Aleyn and John Roth. Edward's grandson, Richard II, favoured courtiers for their culture and talents rather than for their ancestry. Such men would be anxious to show that they possessed qualities of *gentillesse* just as much as the traditional nobility. They were not alone: Chaucer himself was a product of an upwardly-mobile family, and his views on *gentillesse* as a consequence of virtuous living rather than something inherited from a particular blood-line recur with frequency in his writings. In an increasingly fluid society the old belief in a static population, divided into three estates, was fast dissolving. A law of 1363 stipulated that a merchant worth £1000 could wear clothes and eat meals of the same quality as a knight worth £500. Gower wrote: 'the chivalric aristocracy is being replaced by a financial aristocracy; knights have become greedy for money, now fight only for ransom and engage in trade rather than seeking military prowess'. It was left to prosperous, wealthy merchants, landowners and franklins to prove they were the new 'gentlemen'.

▶ What evidence do you find in any of your reading of Chaucer of individuals challenging their accepted role in society? Is this challenge applauded or satirised by the writer?

The Catholic church in the fourteenth century

If the fortunes of ordinary English people seemed less stable during the fourteenth century, it might be felt that security could still be found in the church. The Catholic church was hugely influential in every aspect of medieval life. Everyone belonged to the same church; everyone recognised its power. Each village had its parish priest, each diocese its bishop or archbishop; the overall head of the church was the Pope. Influence was felt not just in spiritual matters, but also in economic, political and legal areas. Monks and nuns lived in religious communities, which were often very wealthy. (Friars also belonged to religious communities, but traditionally they travelled far and wide, dispensing religious instruction, and accepting alms from the towns and villages they visited, as they went.) Healing of the sick was largely in the hands of the monasteries and nunneries, which also offered shelter to travellers and succour for the needy. They were centres of learning too; most early fourteenth century schools were attached to monastic orders; education was in the hands of the church, as were the great libraries of Europe. The term 'clerk' meant a literate man, and literacy was, by and large, a skill associated with churchmen. A growing number of the aristocracy enjoyed reading and writing, but one did not need to be able to read in order to handle a sword or a horse. In monastic cells throughout Christendom, before printing was available, books were manuscript, usually copied painstakingly onto parchment or vellum, often exquisitely decorated. Although there were many collections of stories, histories and fables not related to religion, much of what the monks produced was obviously religious in content.

Many might envy the quiet life of a scribe, but it had some drawbacks, most eloquently described here by Hoccleve, the poet, who worked as a clerk all his life. He pictures himself looking wistfully out of his window at the cheerful life going on outside:

> Thys artificers se I day by day
> In the hootteste of al hyre bysynesse
> Talken and singe and make game and play
> And forth hyr labour passyth wyth gladnesse,
> But we laboure in travayllous stilnesse:
> We stowpe and stare upon the schepys skyn
> And kepe must oure song and wordys in.

> *I see these workmen*
> *in the midst of their hardest work*
> *chatting, singing and messing about*
> *and their hard work goes on happily;*
> *but we work in burdensome silence:*

we stoop and peer at the parchment
and must stop ourselves from singing or chatting.

Writing, he said, brings about three ailments: bending over a manuscript all day was bad for the stomach, dreadful for the back, but most particularly it ruined the eyesight.

▶ 'Clerks' figure largely in Chaucer's *Canterbury Tales*. Would you expect Chaucer to be sympathetic towards them?

The church owned huge estates, possibly a third of the land and wealth of the country. Many labourers spent their lives governed by the church both spiritually and economically, since the very fields they worked and the villages they inhabited were on church lands. The largest and most impressive buildings they saw were great abbeys and cathedrals, designed and built by ambitious, often over-extravagant prelates. Drama and colour in their lives came from church services, religious processions and mystery plays, decorated church interiors and dramatic sermons. In theory this was a satisfying and comforting situation; in practice there was considerable discontent and bewilderment about the role of the Catholic church in the fourteenth century. As the concept of the nation state grew throughout Europe, political rulers began to object to the amount of influence the church held over its population. The church ran its own legal courts and collected its own taxes, often claiming exemption from taxes levied by princes.

▶ How might Chaucer's attitude to the church have been affected by his social status and position as a poet writing for a courtly audience? You might find the extracts in Part 3 from *The Pardoner's Tale* and *The Summoner's Tale* useful here.

The Papal Schism

Economic and political rivalry between France and the Papacy in the early fourteenth century had developed into a power struggle; Clement V, a French pope, chose to set up a new papal court in Avignon, close to the protective influence of the French king. This provided a base for a succession of popes increasingly worldly in outlook – it became the 'Babylon of the West' according to Petrarch. Although the Papacy returned to Rome in 1377, bishops were unable to agree in their choice of religious leader in the papal elections, and two rival candidates claimed the title of pope. This split or schism disrupted the unity of the Catholic church and had a devastating effect on its status. Countries chose which side to support for political not religious reasons. The rival claimants fought to establish themselves in costly wars during which money-making practices of all kinds flourished: sales of pardons and indulgences increased, as did the practice of selling benefices (church offices) to the highest bidders; the purchase and display of holy relics for commercial gain grew, and new chantries (or chapels) were built, where, for a price, ceaseless prayers provided intercession for souls in purgatory (the souls of the dead enduring the miseries of this antechamber to Hell until they had paid sufficient penalty for their sins).

▶ Compare two religious characters from *The General Prologue*. How worldly or spiritual are they, and to what extent does Chaucer admire or criticise each one?

Undoubtedly there were many devout and trustworthy churchmen, but lax moral values became the subject of satirists and cynics everywhere. In particular, the idea of celibacy in monks, friars and members of the priesthood was ridiculed. In a world where popes famously had mistresses and children, how could this be otherwise? Medieval literature abounds with references to amorous churchmen. Chaucer's *Shipman's Tale* concerns a friar who pays one hundred franks in order to spend the night with the beautiful, but grasping, wife of his 'good friend'. William Langland describes a similar character – a 'limitour' [a friar who has been given a licence enabling him to ask for alms at any house within a specified area]:

> I knewe such oon ones, nat eyhte wynter passed,
> Cam ynne thus ycoped at a court ther I dwelte,
> And was my lordes leche and my ladyes bothe.
> And at the laste this lymytour, tho my lord was oute,
> He salved so oure wymmen til some were with childe!

> *I knew a friar like him, less than eight winters ago*
> *arrived in a fine cloak at the court where I lived,*
> *and made love to both my lord and my lady.*
> *And in the end, when my lord was away*
> *he 'saved' the women in such a way he left them pregnant!*

It is ironic that the most unpleasant character in *The Canterbury Tales* is the Pardoner, who cares not at all for spiritual values, but is justifiably proud of his skills as a preacher because of the financial benefit they bring from gullible audiences hungry for some sort of spiritual comfort and enlightenment.

▶ Is it possible to discern in Chaucer's writings a serious note about the absence of spiritual values in contemporary society? Read the passage from *Retractions* in Part 3 on page 92.

Anti-clericalism and reform

People of all ranks felt an urgent longing to find some sort of new contact with God, not necessarily through conventional church teaching. They turned elsewhere for spiritual, moral and intellectual stimulus, particularly during the years of the Black Death, when comfort and reassurance were desperately needed. To many it seemed God's anger had been brought about by the deficiencies in his church on earth. Mystics, such as Julian of Norwich, who spoke of direct contact between the individual and God, were widely admired. The pain and misery brought about by sin, said Julian, exist only:

> for a tyme, for it purgyth and makyth us to know oureselfe and aske mercy; for the passion of oure Lorde is comfort to us ayenst alle thys, and so is his blessyd wylle. And for the tender love that oure good Lorde hath to alle that shall be savyd, he comfortyth redely and swetly, menyng thus: 'It is true that synne is cause of alle thys payne, but alle shall be wele, and alle maner of thyng shall be wele.'

Despite the church's best endeavours to denounce various branches of study as evil, interest in magic and astronomy grew. Forbidden by the church to practise anatomy and dissection, medical men put their trust in the theory of mankind governed by a balance of four humours, and the positions of the constellations in the sky, for each sign of the zodiac was seen to control particular parts of the body. Dates and times were also calculated according to the position of planets. A splendid example of this reckoning can be found in the introduction to *The Man of Law's Tale:*

> Oure Hooste saugh wel that the brighte sonne
> The ark of his artificial day hath ronne
> The ferthe part, and half an houre and moore,
> And though he were nat depe ystert in loore,
> He wiste it was the eightetethe day
> Of Aprill, that is messager to May;
> and saugh wel that the shadwe of every tree
> Was as in lengthe the same quantitee
> That was the body erect that caused it.
> And therfore by the shadwe he took his wit
> That Phebus, which that shoon so clere and brighte,
> Degrees was fyve and fourty clombe on highte;
> And for that day, as in that latitude,
> It was ten of the clokke, he gan conclude,

> *Our Host saw that the bright sun*
> *had travelled through the curved route of his working day*
> *a quarter, and over half an hour more,*
> *and, though not an expert in this knowledge,*

he knew it was the eighteenth day
of April, that heralds May
and he saw each tree's shadow
was the same length and size
as the tree itself
And so he used his intelligence to calculate
that the sun, which shone so bright and clear,
had climbed to an altitude of forty five degrees
And for that day, as in that latitude,
he worked out that it was ten o'clock.

Similar calculations were to be found in a famous book, *Kalendarium,* by Nicholas of Lynn. The particular planets in the ascendant on high were believed to have significant effects on events on the earth below, and on the behaviour of people. The Wife of Bath blamed her particular blend of aggression and amorousness on the influence of Mars and Venus. Knowledgeable as many were about the use of herbs and plants, when these failed to cure men turned to old wives' tales and magic. The aftermath of the Black Death saw increasing need for the comfort of belief in saints, and, less admirably, superstitious prejudice against particular minorities in society, such as Jews. The importance of Fate, or Fortune, figured largely in medieval attitudes – the idea that human life was governed by some larger, hidden plan, and that each individual was somehow helpless in the face of a predestined future.

But there was also a feeling that the Catholic church had proved inadequate in the face of such catastrophic times, and, as people travelled more widely, they became more aware of the world and spoke out more critically and openly against the faults they perceived in the clergy. In a fast-changing world, the church seemed grimly determined to hang on to the privileges and attitudes of the past, regardless of growing evidence of its deficiencies.

Education and the growth of literacy – new ideas

Little encouragement had been given towards developing literacy in those not intending to go into the church, but the dangerous decline in scholars after the Black Death (since plague spread like wildfire within close-packed monastic communities) coincided with an upsurge of interest in educational establishments not exclusively tied to church interests. In 1382 William of Wykeham founded Winchester, a school for secular clerks so magnificent that it became the model for all public schools that followed. Up to four hundred grammar schools were set up around the country, where clever boys of poor birth could study and become clerks – a good opportunity for young men of humble family to better themselves. Nevertheless, this extract from a manuscript in Balliol College, Oxford shows that then, as now, students were often reluctant to go to school – especially on Monday mornings:

> I wold fayn be a clarke,
> But yet hit is a strange werke;
> The byrchyn twygges be so sharpe
> Hit makith me have a faynt harte.
>
> On Monday in the mornyng whan I shall rise
> At six of the clok hyt is the gise
> To go to skole withowt avise –
> I had lever go twenti myle twyse!
>
> *I'd like to become a clerk,*
> *but it's difficult work.*
> *The birch twigs bite so keenly* [when he's beaten]
> *that it makes me become quite downhearted.*
>
> *On Monday mornings, when I have to get up*
> *at six o'clock, as happens every day,*
> *and set off for school without any question* [or objection]
> *I'd rather walk twenty miles!*

After grammar school, study continued at the universities of Oxford and Cambridge. These universities were lively places, teaching the seven basic roots of medieval study: Grammar, Logic, Rhetoric, Arithmetic, Geometry, Music and, noblest of all, Astronomy, which was connected with divinity and theology, from which all other study developed. Many universities or colleges became famous for specific branches of learning: the law school of Bologna, the theology teaching in Paris. In England Merton College, Oxford, was the centre for mathematical, scientific and astronomical study, and Chaucer's clerk, Nicolas, in *The Miller's Tale,* is an Oxford student, who adorns his lodgings most impressively with astrolabe and astronomical books.

Increasingly, clerks found employment quite outside the church jurisdiction. Some rebellious students clashed with more traditional elements within the university. There was also frequent conflict between town youths and students. In 1354 Oxford university temporarily closed down after a brawl resulting in the death of considerable numbers of clerks and students; townsmen, rallying to the cry of 'stryke herde and give goode knockes', disposed of the bodies of at least sixty students in the town dunghill. In 1381 students rioting in Cambridge destroyed university charters and records.

▶ What reasons might there have been for such rivalry between town and gown? Look at the ways in which Chaucer presents this rivalry in both *The Miller's Tale* and *The Reeve's Tale*. Notice what the friar says about uneducated people in the passage from *The Summoner's Tale* on page 88 in Part 3.

John Wyclif and the Lollards

Fierce debates abounded between conventional church scholars and more radical thinkers. In particular, John Wyclif, Master of Balliol, became a focus for much discontent. He valued a free and questioning academic life exempt from intrusion and interference from church and Pope. Distressed at the evidence he saw of increases in church land and property, he challenged the payment of revenue by the church in England to the papacy. His early teaching – that spiritual matters belonged to God, but that material issues were the concern of princes – found favour with his political rulers in the 1360s; he became the King's chaplain and found a strong ally in John of Gaunt, Duke of Lancaster. But when he pursued his ideas further, towards their logical conclusion, saying that no man, priest or layman, could be seen as 'better' or more powerful than another, he alarmed the ruling classes. By 1379 he was promoting the rejection of a corrupt papacy, and a reformed church controlled by the king. When he also questioned the truth of one of the primary concepts of the Catholic church, transubstantiation [the belief that bread and wine literally become the body and blood of Christ during the Mass], he came to be seen as a revolutionary threat to the secular as well as the church establishment. Dismay at the turmoil and despair created by the Papal Schism had brought Wyclif to the brink of challenging the autonomy of the Catholic church.

▶ From the paragraph above make a note of the aspects of religious practice Wyclif approved of, and those he criticised, and read the extracts on page 81 from *The Pardoner's Tale,* on page 88 from *The Summoner's Tale* and page 92 from Chaucer's *Retractions*. From what you read, does it seem possible that Chaucer sympathised with Wyclif?

There were many who endorsed some, if not all, of Wyclif's ideas. The Lollards, under Wyclif's guidance, produced a Bible translated into English and thus more accessible to all strata of society (since Latin remained the language used in churches). Although all copies of his Bible were later ordered to be destroyed (merely owning a copy could result in a charge of heresy) nearly two hundred copies still survive – an indication, perhaps, of how many originally existed. For the first time, English people were able to hear or read the book absolutely fundamental to their faith in their own language:

If I speke with tungis *[tongues]* of men and of aungels, and I have not charite, I am maad as bras sownynge *[sounding brass]* or a symbale tynkynge. And if I have prophecie, and knowe alle mysteries and al kunnyng *[knowledge]*, and if I have al feith so that I move hillis fro her place, and I have not charite, I am nought. And if I departe *[give]* alle my goodis into the metis of pore men, and if I bitake my bodi so that I brenne *[burn]*, and if I have not charite, it profitith to me nothing. Charite is pacient; it is benygne. Charite envyeth not. It doith not wickidli *[does no wickedness]*. It is not blowun *[conceited]*. It is not coveitous. It sekith not the thingis that ben his owne. It is not stirid to wrathe. It thenkith not yvel *[evil]*. It joyeth not on wickidnesse, but it joyeth togidere to treuthe. It suffrith alle thingis. It bileveth alle thingis. It hopith alle thingis. It susteyneth alle thingis.

▶ Compare the passage above with the equivalent passage (Corinthians 1 verse 13) from a modern Bible. Which seems to you a) to give the clearer message, b) to sound more attractive? Consider rhythm, language and clarity as you justify your views.

Wyclif's was the inspiration behind much free-thinking and emphasis on individual rights and responsibilities characteristic of attitudes of the 1380s. Certainly stimulus for discontent came from his teaching, erupting in 1381 into the most potentially dangerous civil rebellion of the century.

1381 – The Peasants' Revolt

Criticism of oppressive church authority, particularly the power and wealth of the monasteries, was growing by the late fourteenth century; even in quiet rural areas ordinary people were stirred by the preaching of the Lollards, who travelled the length of the country spreading their ideas. Men like John Ball, a rebel priest from York, worked tirelessly teaching a revolutionary, democratic view of the world. An unpopular and oppressive poll tax brought things to a head. On 11 June 1381, Wat Tyler led his disciplined and effective army from Canterbury, to camp within two days on Blackheath. Another group from Essex were at Mile End, outside Aldgate. Geoffrey Chaucer, living in the house beside the gate at that time, would almost certainly have seen them as they marched up Southwark, and again when they marched out to meet the king a few days later. Amongst Richard II's supporters at that time was Chaucer's neighbour and close acquaintance, Nicholas Brembre, later Lord Mayor. Londoners, sympathetic to the rebels' cause, opened the city gates, and a bloody and frightening few days ensued. Flemish weavers were massacred and their beheaded bodies left in Thames Street, near Chaucer's house. Prisoners were released from the Marshalsea and Fleet Prisons, ecclesiastical and legal records were destroyed and London Bridge was taken, ensuring free access for rebels in and out of the city. John of Gaunt's magnificent Savoy palace was burned to the ground, all the Bishop of Lichfield's fine wines were drunk and the Archbishop of Canterbury was beheaded on Tower Hill. Richard II, then fourteen, his mother and his chief advisers took refuge in the Tower, before that too was ransacked.

With extraordinary personal bravery Richard agreed to meet Tyler and other leaders at Smithfield, on 15 June, in full view of the rebel forces. During this meeting Wat Tyler was pulled from his horse and killed by one of Richard's men. The rebels' mood turned from possible appeasement to fury, but, riding forward to confront them, Richard apparently shouted 'Sirs, would you shoot your king? I am your leader now!' He promised free pardons for those who dispersed peacefully. Without Tyler's leadership they were 'like sheep' and the uprising lost its impetus. Richard's promises proved meaningless. Ringleaders were executed or imprisoned, and stringent measures taken to restore the *status quo*. 'Villeins ye are and villeins ye shall remain,' threatened the young king, once the danger had passed. All hint of revolt quashed, the old order persisted, both in state and church. Such firmly established powers and such deeply ingrained beliefs were not obliterated easily, though dissatisfaction rumbled beneath the surface.

This is a modern transcript of John Ball's speech to the peasant army camped at Blackheath:

> All you good people, matters go not well in England, nor shall they till everything be in common; and there be no villeins [*labourers*] nor gentlemen, but we are all united together; and the lords be no greater than we. What have we deserved, why should we be kept thus in servitude? We are all from one father and mother, Adam and Eve: how can they say or show that they are greater than us? They make us labour for their benefit. They are clothed in velvet and fur and we are dressed in poor cloth; they have their wines, spices and good bread, and we have only the chaff and drink water; they dwell in fair houses, and we have the pain and effort, the rain and wind in the fields. We are called their bondsmen, and if we do not readily give them service, we are beaten. Let us go to the king, he is young, and show him what servitude we are in, and show him how we would have it otherwise.

John Ball was executed on 15 July 1381.

▶ Chaucer makes only one direct reference to the uprising, a reticence perhaps explained by his position at court. In *The Nun's Priest's Tale* he compares the rebels chasing and killing Flemish weavers in London to the pursuit of a wily fox by an outraged mob of villagers. How does the tone of this comparison indicate his possible attitude to the revolt?

They yolleden as feendes doon in helle;
The dokes cryden as men wolde hem quelle;
The gees for feere flowen over the trees;
Out of the hive cam the swarm of bees.
So hidous was the noise, a, benedicitee!
Certes, he Jakke Straw and his meynee
Ne made nevere shoutes half so shrille
Whan that they wolden any Fleming kille,
As thilke day was maad upon the fox.

They yelled like devils in hell;
the ducks cried as if they were being killed;
the terrified geese flew over the trees;
out of their hive came a swarm of bees.
God bless us, the noise was so awful,
truly, even Jack Straw [rebel leader] and his gang
never made half such shrill shouts
when they were killing the Flemings
as were made in the outcry this day about the fox.

Women's place in society

One way in which the church continued to assert authority in society was in the anti-feminine teaching that emanated from many pulpits and manuscripts of the fourteenth century. A thirteenth century Dominican monk, Vincent de Beauvais, called womankind 'the confusion of man, an insatiable beast, a continuous anxiety, an incessant warfare, a daily ruin, a house of tempest, a hindrance to devotion'. The church's stance was that women were certainly inferior to, and often the ruin of, men. In *The Canterbury Tales* Chaucer suffered the Wife of Bath to repeat many of the common criticisms levelled at women in the writings of male theologians and triumphantly to refute them, though her arguments and behaviour can themselves be seen as proof of the anti-feminists' argument. Medieval literature abounded with the stock characters of anti-feminist literature – the unfaithful wife, the harridan, the gossip, the deceiver of blindly adoring husbands, the money-grabbing harlot. So much emphasis was laid on urging women to be meek, obedient and respectful to their husbands that it might be suspected that the opposite was often the case.

This was, nonetheless, only one perspective. If Eve was one symbol of female character, the Virgin Mary was another. Just as the mother of Christ was revered and sanctified by all devout Christians, so, went the thinking, good women – pure virgins and loving mothers – should be accorded similar treatment. This reverence, adoration even, formed the basis of the elaborate, romantic elevation of women that formed the central theme of the game of courtly love. The fantasy world of romance, widely celebrated in contemporary literature and art, had developed from the ideas of chivalry promoted as behaviour that distinguished gentlemen from commoners. Young men, like the Squire in Chaucer's *General Prologue,* would expect to suffer pangs of unrequited love as a more or less permanent and painful condition. The beloved was traditionally out of reach, either because she was an untouchable virgin, or the virtuous wife of another man. Like Chaucer's Squire, all a young man could do was write songs, sing, fight and joust to the best of his ability, and behave always in a manner of perfect chivalry or *gentillesse* 'in hope to stonden in his lady grace'. This literary convention of the pining lover and the anguish of unrequited love may be found in literature from any century.

▶ Compare the despair captured in the first lines of Chaucer's *Parlement of Fowles* with the subsequent lines from Book 4 of Gower's *Confessio Amantis* in which the passive and helpless state of the lover is used to illustrate the sin of Idleness or Sloth:

> The lyf so short, the craft so long to lerne,
> Th'assay so hard, so sharp the conquerynge,
> The dredful joye alwey that slit so yerne:
> Al this mene I by Love, that my felynge
> Astonyeth with his wonderful werkynge
> So sore, iwis, that whan I on hym thynke
> Nat wot I wel wher that I flete or synke.
>
> *(Parlement of Fowles)*

> *Life is so short, this art takes so long to learn,*
> *the painful struggle, the difficult conquest,*
> *the fearful joy that vanishes so fast –*
> *all this is what I mean by Love, so that my feelings*
> *are amazed by his strange operations.*
> *I am so wounded, I know, that when I think of Love*
> *I don't know whether I sink or swim.*

> What so mi lady hath me bede,
> With al myn herte obedient
> I have therto be diligent.
> And if so is sche bidde noght,
> What thing that thanne into my thoght
> Comth ferst of that I mai suffise,
> I bowe and profre my servise,
> Somtime in chambre, somtime in halle,
> Riht as I se the times falle.
> And whan sche goth to hiere masse,

That time schal noght overpasse
That I n'aproche hir ladihede
In aunter if I mai hire lede
Unto the chapelle and ayein.
Thanne is noght al mi weie in vein,

(Confessio Amantis)

Whatever my lady has asked of me
I obey with all my heart,
I have done my best to obey.
And, if she asks nothing of me,
whatever then comes to my mind
first of all, that I might be able to perform
I bow and offer to do this service.
Sometimes in the bower, sometimes in the great hall,
wherever I see the time might be right.
And when she goes to hear mass in church,
that time shall not pass by
without my approaching her ladyship
in case I may escort her
to the chapel and back again.
Then my journey has not been in vain.

Common sense suggests that the reality was very different from these two extremes. Women were, in many ways, second class citizens in the fourteenth century. Few were given the education available to men, for the majority of schools were still run by monks, and all catered exclusively for boys. Even girls born into noble families received education largely restricted to home economics, sewing, French, singing, dancing and manners. Only in exceptional circumstances did women gain status on their own account: there is record of a woman practising medicine in Paris in 1322 (though without qualifications), and a woman don, Novella d'Andrea, lectured at the University of Bologna in the 1360s, her face hidden by a veil lest her undergraduate students should be distracted by her beauty. The literary world was dominated by men, but one powerful and talented woman made her mark as a professional writer: Christine de Pisan, widowed at 25 in 1389, supported herself and her young children through her writings, which became enormously popular in her native France and abroad. Her book *La Cité des Dames* was uniquely and importantly a book about women by a woman.

▶ Women's voices in literature were very few. Chaucer allowed many of his women characters a strong voice. Look at the passages on pages 82-3, 85 and 91 in Part 3. How convincing are the female characters created here?

Although women like Mme de Pisan were exceptions, doubtless in all walks of life some women were both forceful and influential. Peasant women could hold tenancies of land in their own right (though they were paid less than their male counterparts for their labour); women were traditionally in the majority in such areas of commerce as spinning and brewing, and widows frequently plied some trade independently if they did not re-marry. The 'povre widwe' in Chaucer's *Nun's Priest's Tale* leads a simple, but clearly contented life:

> Thre large sowes hadde she, and namo.
> Thre keen, and eek a sheep that highte Malle.
> Ful sooty was hire bour and eek hir halle,
> In which she eet ful many a sklendre meel.
> Of poynaunt sauce hir neded never a deel.
> No deyntee morsel passed thurgh hir throte;
> Hir diet was accordant to hir cote.

> *She had three large sows, and no more,*
> *three cows and a sheep called Malle.*
> *Her bedroom was very sooty, and so was her main room*
> *where she ate many a frugal meal.*
> *She needed no tasty sauces.*
> *No delicacies passed down her throat;*
> *her diet was in keeping with her cottage home.*

► What is the effect of using words like 'bower' and 'halle' – more suited to describing the home of a great lady than a humble cottage? Read the passage in Part 3 from *The Nun's Priest's Tale* and consider why the widow's cockerel is treated in a similar manner.

Wealthy middle-class wives ran large households, controlling several servants, handling their husbands' business accounts, disciplining apprentices and taking responsibility for basic nursing and medical attention required by the household. Such duties were also taken on by the wives of knights, on an even larger scale. In addition, if their husbands were away from home, fighting in the king's wars, or maybe attending court, it would often fall upon the lady of the household not merely to manage household matters, but also to take control of the administration of her lord's estates. Unmarried well-born ladies might become nuns, and, like Chaucer's Prioress, be responsible for the discipline and organisation of a convent. Criseyde sums up her independent status in an intriguingly modern way:

> I am myn owene womman, wel at ese –
> I thank it God – as after myn estat,
> Right yong, and stonde unteyd in lusty leese,

Withouten jalousie or swich debat:
Shal noon housbond seyn to me 'Chek mat!'
For either they ben ful of jalousie,
Or maisterfull, or loven novelrie.

I am my own woman, and comfortable with that -
thank God – as is fitting to my status,
I'm young, and uninvolved in any physical attachment,
not hampered by jealousy or any such thing:
no husband shall tell me what to do
either because they're full of jealousy
or bossy or enjoy the novelty of mastery.

▶ Do the excerpts above suggest that male writers of the fourteenth century are guilty of stereotyping women characters?

Assignments

1   Using evidence from one or more of *The Canterbury Tales,* and any other textual information at your disposal, discuss the view that Chaucer understood and was sympathetic towards women.

2   Looking back at the passages included in this section, what reasons can you find for the enduring popularity of Chaucer's works, whilst many other writers of his time are far less known? Can you make out a case for reading fourteenth century literature (apart from passing examinations)?

3   Voltaire said: 'History never repeats itself, man always does.' Choose the description of any one of Chaucer's pilgrims from *The Canterbury Tales,* and consider what information you glean from it of a life lived according to procedures very different from our own, and also what characteristics of behaviour and conduct are recognisable today.

4   Attempt to write a modern character study along the lines of those in *The General Prologue.* Try to imitate Chaucer's method of pointing out faults without apparently criticising them. What do you learn from this exercise?

5   Using the characters presented in *The General Prologue,* consider how
    Chaucer sometimes creates individuals who are at odds with their social
    or occupational position.

6   Make your own brief summary of the main events and aspects of life
    which seem to have been most important in the fourteenth century. How
    many of these can be said to be relevant today?

7   By looking back over the passages included in this section, and some
    from Part 3, (particularly the extract from *The Miller's Tale* and the
    anonymous song about the cockerel), decide how much the style of
    writing was affected by the type of audience for which it was intended.

8   Chaucer has been described as a satirist and a humorous writer. Is it still
    possible to appreciate his satire and his humour today?

9   How much have Chaucer's subject matter and style been affected by the
    audience for whom he wrote? Use evidence from this section, as well as
    passages from Part 3 to illustrate your answer.

10 What seems to have been Chaucer's attitude to the church and to church
    officials?

2 | Approaching the texts

- Looking at the language: how much is this a problem?

- How effectively did a sense of 'English' style develop in the fourteenth century? What were its roots?

- What were the sources most frequently used by Chaucer and his contemporaries?

- What genres, or types of literature, were common in the fourteenth century? How were these parodied and re-worked?

Dialect and 'Standard English'

Although there were wide variations between the dialects of different regions in the fourteenth century, a common core of 'established' English existed, particularly in the area between Oxford, Cambridge and London: the two seats of learning and the political and commercial centre. This was the English used at court and by the Chancery clerks whose government records deliberately ironed out regional differences in grammar and vocabulary, thus producing a 'Standard English' accessible throughout the country. This was the language used by Chaucer, Londoner and court poet, and the language adopted in 1476 by Caxton, when he established his printing press at Westminster.

Reading Chaucer

Although the language Chaucer used initially seems discouragingly different from contemporary English, this need not make the enjoyment of fourteenth century texts an impossible experience.

First, get some idea of the general subject matter of a passage. Modern readers are not usually expected to struggle with a piece of old manuscript – Chaucer is presented on a clearly printed page, well punctuated. Even if the edition you use does not give you some idea of what is going on, there are usually words you recognise as familiar. Break the passage down into sentences, and deal with one sentence at a time.

Here are the first few lines of *The Knight's Tale*. How much can you understand from a first reading? You will probably find it helpful to try reading the passage aloud.

> Whilom, as olde stories tellen us,
> Ther was a duc that highte Theseus;

Of Atthenes he was lord and governour,
And in his time swich a conquerour
That gretter was ther noon under the sonne.
Ful many a riche contree hadde he wonne;
What with his wisdom and his chivalrie,
He conquered al the regne of Femenye,
That whilom was ycleped Scithia,
And weddede the queen Ypolita,
And broghte hire hoom with him in his contree
With muchel glorie and greet solempnitee,
And eek hir yonge suster Emelye.

Reading out loud becomes less embarrassing when you remember that no one can be completely certain how medieval English was spoken, and that there were considerable differences in pronunciation in various parts of the country. As you read you will find that many words sound quite similar to their modern equivalents, but are spelt differently: common sense suggests that *duc,* for instance, is likely to mean 'duke', and *contree* possibly translates as 'country'. You will notice that many words end with an extra 'e' or double consonant plus 'e': *sonne* [sun], and *wonne* [won], as well as *broghte* [brought] and *yonge* [young]. Generally speaking, a 'y' at the start of a word is pronounced as in 'party', and the combination of the vowels 'gh' [as in *broghte*] would sound like the Scots 'ch' in 'loch'. The rhythm of the verse (in this case iambic pentameter) should help you to work out how many syllables are in each line; you sound or omit the 'e' at the ends of words as necessary. For instance, in order to achieve ten syllables in each of the first two lines of this passage, the final 'e' will have to be sounded in both *olde* and *highte.*

▶ Try reading the passage again, making an effort to maintain the strong metrical structure Chaucer employed here and in many of his other works. Are there any lines where alternative readings are possible? (For more ideas of how the language might have sounded, listen to the tapes of Chaucer published by the Cambridge University Press; see page 123, Part 6.)

There are still some words in the passage that may seem difficult. Some occur so frequently in medieval English that you will quickly learn them: *whilom* [once upon a time], *highte* [called, known as], *swych* [such] and *eek* [also]. The word *hem* frequently, but not always, means 'them'. A 'y' at the beginning of a verb usually denotes the passive state: here the phrase *was ycleped* means 'was named'. Other words can be guessed from the context – *suster* [sister], *gretter* [greater] and *muchel* [much]. A glossary or an annotated edition will give additional helpful information – for example, that *solempnitee* means not seriousness but dignity and splendour, and that the *regne of Femenye* is the kingdom of women, or Amazons, where the legendary duke, Theseus, met and married Hippolyta.

▶ You will have noticed that the passage is written in rhyming couplets. What are the advantages of this style in a piece of work likely to be read aloud?

▶ There are three rhyming lines at the end of this passage, rather than the usual two. Might this suggest something about the content of the final line?

The roots of English poetry

Most writings that survive from earlier centuries are in Latin. They were the work of scholars like the great Northumbrian monk, the Venerable Bede (673–735), who chose Latin for his *Historia Ecclesiastica Gentis Anglorum* [Ecclesiastical History of the English People] because it was the language of all scholars of the Christian world, and thus the great unifying bond of the Catholic church.

There are a few texts written in the vernacular (known as Old English) which remain, two of the most important being Beowulf and the writings of Caedmon.

Caedmon (died *c.* 670)

An illiterate, inspired poet and herdsman, Caedmon lived at Whitby Abbey, part of the great northern kingdom of Northumbria, a Christian stronghold. He spoke of the creation of the world, in language which combined all the fervour of a newly Christianised society with the fierce, warlike attitudes of Anglo-Saxon society. Describing God creating Hell, for instance, he pictured him like a warlord bent on revenging himself on the rebel angels.

Beowulf

Possibly written in the eighth century, and preserved in a manuscript from the tenth century, this anonymous poem, written in Old English, celebrates the life of fighting men, united in their companionship in times of hardship. *Beowulf* praises the virtues of loyalty and stoicism when faced with disasters and fearsome enemies. Women play very little part in this world. As in the earlier verses of Caedmon, the use of alliteration, assonance and pronounced rhythms indicates that this was a work to be recited rather than read. Old English poetry relied heavily on assonance, rather than rhyme, with long lines divided by a break or caesura into two half-lines, which emphasised stressed words by use of alliteration.

▶ Read the two extracts below, from Caedmon's hymns of praise and from the moment in *Beowulf* when the hero with his men arrives to assist Hrothgar, the Danish king, in driving out the fearful monster, Grendel. Both have been rendered into modern English, whilst trying to retain the rhythms and mood of the original, as well as much of the vocabulary.

Now must we greet with praise the guard of Heaven's realm,
The Maker's might, and of his mind the thought,
The glorious Father's works, and how to wonders all
He gave beginning, He, the Eternal Lord!
He at the very first formed for the bairns of men,
He, Holy Shaper! Heaven for their roof;
Then Middle-garth He made: He, of mankind the Ward!
Lord everlasting He! And then He let arise
The earth for man; He is Almighty God!

(Caedmon)

So they duly arrived
in their grim war-graith and gear at the hall,
and, weary from the sea, stacked wide shields
of the toughest hardwood against the wall,
then collapsed on the benches; battle-dress
and weapons clashed. They collected their spears
in a seafarers' stook, a stand of greyish
tapering ash. And the troops themselves
were as good as their weapons.

Then a proud warrior
questioned the men concerning their origins:
'Where do you come from, carrying these
decorated shields and shirts of mail,
these cheek-hinged helmets and javelins?
I am Hrothgar's herald and officer.
I have never seen so impressive or large
an assembly of strangers. Stoutness of heart,
bravery not banishment, must have brought you to Hrothgar.'

(Beowulf)

▶ Compare these passages with the opening lines of *The Canterbury Tales* on page 8. How much do you learn of the concerns and preoccupations of these three authors?

▶ Look at the passages from *Sir Gawain and the Green Knight* and *The Knight's Tale* which appear in Part 3. What similarities do you find in the subject matter of these and the piece from *Beowulf?*

The French influence

After the Norman conquest the position of French as the language of polite society and of culture persisted for over three hundred years. In 1352 an English chronicler, Ranulf Higden, spoke of the decline in the use of English, since children of gentlemen were taught to speak French from the time they were 'yrokked in here cradel', and even those who were not of gentle birth did their best to learn French as a social asset. Even though the rebirth of the English language had already begun, themes and topics dominating English literature during Chaucer's lifetime were largely influenced by French poets. Furthermore, since the late twelfth and thirteenth centuries there had been an enormous increase in the influence of Anglo-Norman vocabulary on Old English. Words connected with law and order, religion, science and scholarship and all aspects of leisured and cultured living were introduced, such as: authority, government, royal, sovereign, justice, pardon, besiege, combat, dinner, feast, olive, roast, salad, beauty, conversation, dalliance, melody, romance, medicine, surgeon, chamber, curtain, cushion.

Where both old and new words continue to be used, there is often a subtle difference in meaning. For example, consider the following pairs (the older English word is always placed first): 'ruth' and 'pity'; 'house' and 'mansion'; 'hearty' and 'cordial'; 'doom' and 'judgement', 'stench' and 'aroma'.

The subject matter of French literature popular in the fourteenth century influenced many writers, Chaucer included. Romance poetry had flourished since the twelfth century, when Eleanor of Aquitaine held court in Poitiers, where troubadours competed for prizes for the best songs and lyrics. She brought her love of music and literature with her when she married Henry Plantagenet, later Henry II of England, and her daughter, Marie de Champagne, displayed similarly cultured tastes. Works from this period were as popular in England as in France. Many of the Arthurian legends re-told in the fourteenth century derived from French versions of the tales; works such as *Sir Gawain and the Green Knight* owe more to French stories of Arthur and his court – Lancelot, Galahad, Merlin, Gawain and so forth – than to any English writings.

Developing an 'English' style

It would not have been surprising if Chaucer had written all his works in French. His poetry was intended for an audience undoubtedly fluent in French and acquainted with French literature and its subject matter. French culture was the culture of the English aristocracy, whilst English was the workaday language of commoners. Use of English in all aspects of social and political life was increasing, but for a poet to proclaim himself an 'English poet' was still a bold and surprising move.

In *Troilus and Criseyde* Chaucer apologises, saying he is simply translating from Latin into English a story previously told by an imaginary classical writer,

Lollius. He asks readers not to blame him if any words are 'lame'.

▶ What impression of himself is Chaucer presenting in these lines? Are his words 'feeble' as he suggests? Does the distance of a 'thousand years' make the writing and the writer seem too dated to be admirable?

> Forwhi to every lovere I me excuse,
> That of no sentement I this endite,
> But out of Latyn in my tonge it write.
>
> Wherfore I nyl have neither thank ne blame
> Of al this werk, but prey yow mekely,
> Disblameth me if any word be lame,
> For as myn auctour seyde, so sey I.
> Ek though I speeke of love unfelyngly,
> Ne wondre is, for it nothyng of newe is;
> A blynd man kan nat juggen wel in hewis.
>
> Ye knowe ek that in forme of speche is chaunge
> Withinne a thousand yeer, and wordes tho
> That hadden pris, now wonder nyce and straunge
> Us thinketh hem, and yet thei spake hem so,
> And spedde as wel in love as men now do;

> *And so I apologise to all lovers:*
> *I write this out of no personal feeling*
> *but simply translate from the Latin into my own tongue.*
>
> *For which I desire neither thanks or reproach*
> *for all this work, but humbly pray you*
> *not to blame me if any words are feeble,*
> *I simply write what the author said.*
> *And if I speak unsympathetically of love*
> *it's not surprising, for there's nothing new about it:*
> *a blind man can't describe colours.*
>
> *You also know that language has altered*
> *during the last thousand years, and words used then*
> *that then had value look silly and peculiar now*
> *as we regard them today, and yet that is what they said*
> *and behaved in love just as we do nowadays.*

The English style developing during the fourteenth century combined the alliterative stress derived from Old English tradition with themes and rhyming patterns originating, much more recently, from French literature. Other poets in Chaucer's lifetime would use similar combinations, emphasising one influence or the other, to a greater or lesser degree.

▶ You may already have noticed the strongly alliterative quality of the extracts from *Piers Plowman* and *Sir Gawain and the Green Knight*, reminiscent of the Old English line. But Langland also uses a narrative device popular in French literature, and one frequently used by Chaucer too, the figure of a dreaming narrator as a framework for his protest at the corruption of the world around him and the urgent need for truly Christian behaviour. Read these opening lines to his poem; what differences do you discern between the vocabulary and poetic style of Langland and that of Chaucer?

> In a somur sesoun whan softe was the sonne
> I shope me into shroudes as I a shep were –
> In abite as an heremite unholy of werkes
> Wente forth in the world wondres to here,
> And say many sellies and selkouthe thynges.
> Ac on a May mornyng on Malverne hulles
> Me biful for to slepe, for werynesse of-walked;
> And in a launde as I lay, lened I and slepte,
> And merveylousliche me mette, as I may telle.
> Al the welthe of the world and the wo bothe
> Wynkyng, as hit were, witterliche I seigh hit;
> Of treuthe and tricherye, tresoun and gyle,
> Al I say slepynge, as I shal telle.

> *In the summer, when the sun shone gently,*
> *I dressed myself in a shepherd's clothes –*
> *in the habit of a hermit – though I was no holy man,*
> *set out into the world ready to hear wonders*
> *and to see many marvels and strange things.*
> *And on a May morning on the Malvern hills*
> *I fell asleep, wearied with walking.*
> *And as I lay in a grassy dell, stretched out and asleep,*
> *I dreamt of wonders, as I shall tell,*
> *of both the wealth and the wretchedness of the world.*
> *Truly I saw it, as it were, yet with closed eyes;*
> *true things and treachery, treason and cunning,*
> *I saw all this while asleep, as I shall tell you.*

Here, for comparison, is Chaucer's dreaming narrator, near the beginning of *The Parlement of Fowles:*

The day gan faylen, and the derke nyght,
That reveth bestes from here besynesse,
Berafte me my bok for lak of lyght,
And to my bed I gan me for to dresse,
Fulfyld of thought and busy hevynesse;
For bothe I hadde thyng which that I nolde
And ek I ne hadde that thyng that I wolde.

But fynally my spirit at the laste,
For wery of my labour al the day,
Tok reste, that made me to slepe faste;
And in my slep I mette, as that I lay,
How Affrican, ryght in the selve aray
That Scipion hym say byfore that tyde,
Was come and stod right at my beddes syde.

The day began to fade, and the dark night,
that drags beasts from their activities,
took me from my book, through lack of light,
and I began to prepare for bed,
deep in thought and heavily brooding:
for I possessed those things I did not want
yet lacked the thing I longed for.

But finally, my mind,
over tired by the day's work,
began to relax, and I fell fast asleep;
and in my sleep I dreamt as I lay there
Scipio Africanus, dressed just as
his grandson, Scipio, saw him in earlier times,
had come and stood by my bedside.

Langland's *Piers Plowman* sees visions of a grand pageant of contemporary society
in all its sinfulness and greed, followed by an exploration of the meaning of true
Christianity, Christ's crucifixion and the harrowing of Hell. His poem, deeply felt
and strongly expressed, pleads for a renewal of stringent spiritual values. Chaucer's
Parlement of Fowles is less specific in its message. The opening lines (on page 45)
suggested that the writer's theme would be the agonies and ecstasies of courtly
love, but the poem goes beyond that fashionable, yet sometimes superficial, topic.
The two lines which complete the first stanza quoted above set the tone for a piece
of work which provokes questions from the thoughtful reader, rather than offering
answers.

The subject matter of *Sir Gawain* was undoubtedly influenced by French romance literature, and Gawain was a well-known figure of Arthurian romances. Yet in this work too, the Old English alliterative style plays an important part in the vigour and power of the writing. Poetry from the north-west region frequently employed alliterative stresses in each line to give verse its forceful rhythm. Although this is a subtle and sophisticated poem, it is perhaps easiest to appreciate the force of the alliterative line in the extract below, in which a boar hunt is successfully completed, and the carcass prepared for a triumphant return to the castle. (One eminent medievalist suggests that reading aloud in a broad northern accent – lengthening vowels and sounding all consonants – probably gets some of the effect of a contemporary reading.)

> Fyrst he hewes of his hed and on highe settes,
> And sythen rendes hym al roghe bi the rygge after,
> Braydes out the boweles, brennes hom on glede,
> With bred blent therwith his braches rewardes,
> Sythen he britnes out the brawen in bryght brode sheldes,
> And has out the hastlettes, as hightly bisemes;
> And yet hem halches al hole the halves togeder,
> And sythen on a stif stange stoutly hem henges.

> *First he cuts off its head and sets it on high,*
> *then chops it roughly along the backbone,*
> *pulls out the bowels, roasts them on a hot fire,*
> *mixes them with bread as a treat for the hounds,*
> *then slices the boar flesh into gleaming slabs,*
> *removes the entrails, as is proper;*
> *then fastens the two halves of carcass together*
> *and hangs them on a stout pole.*

▶ Look at the extract on page 93 and consider how effectively the Gawain poet creates a convincing picture of a battle. Does he seem to be saying the same things about warfare as Chaucer is in the description of war on pages 31 and 90?

Chaucer's developing style

Only occasionally does Chaucer choose this strongly alliterative form, more often turning to the sort of metre and rhyme scheme seemingly best adapted to presenting French themes in the English language. Early works, such as *The Boke of the Duchess* and the unfinished *House of Fame,* were written in octosyllabic couplets, the metre used in French poetry. Both of these works present the poet as an observer, wandering through a dream world full of the stories and ideas of great writers of the past.

Chaucer came across the works of Dante in the 1370s, and it seems likely that the Italian's ability to write supreme poetry in his native language – poetry comparable with the greatest classical writers – inspired him to attempt something similar in English. He struggled to find a verse form that suited the natural rhythms of English speech and, finally, in the early 1380s, he began to use the iambic pentameter, a longer line, which seemed to offer infinite scope to a writer of English, and still does. English poets would continue to use it through the centuries:

> Whan that Aprill with his shoures soote
> The droghte of March hath perced to the roote,…

> Shall I compare thee to a summer's day?
> Thou art more lovely and more temperate…
>
> (Shakespeare)

> To do aught good never will be our task,
> But ever to do ill our sole delight…
>
> (John Milton)

> Much have I travell'd in the realms of gold
> And many goodly states and kingdoms seen…
>
> (John Keats)

> Do not go gentle into that good night
> Old age should burn and rave at close of day…
>
> (Dylan Thomas)

Chaucer made the transition to the longer line in *The Parlement of Fowles,* though his subject matter continued to suggest strong allegiance to the French tradition. He combined the ten-syllable line with a verse form known as the 'rhyme royal'– 7-line rhyming stanzas (ababbcc), the stanza form used in *The Man of Law's Tale.* *Troilus and Criseyde* was also written in rhyme royal, appropriately for a long narrative based firmly on a theme from classical literature. The pithy, witty and often satirical tone of many of *The Canterbury Tales* is better suited to rhyming couplets, though Chaucer returned to rhyme royal in some tales, most notably where a serious, thoughtful or even sentimental tone was required.

Medieval source material

> And in this bok were written fables
> That clerkes had in olde tyme,
> And other poetes, put in rime
> To rede…

It is sometimes surprising to modern readers to realise that fourteenth century writers rarely, if ever, attempted to 'make up' stories they wrote. Most literature traced its origins to earlier writings, and poets like Chaucer, who wrote for cultured audiences, expected them to recognise much of the source material being used. Story-telling was a public entertainment, enormously popular, and what was important was the way source material was handled. Nowadays authors usually claim copyright of material they have written themselves. Medieval writers would have found such a concept difficult to understand. Who owned a text, if it was something translated from Latin or Greek into the vernacular? Or if it was a story originally written by Ovid, adapted by an Italian writer, such as Boccaccio, and then translated and adapted yet again by Chaucer? Who was the author of a morality play performed in, say, York or Coventry, if it was developed from a Bible story, with words remembered, enhanced and passed down from generation to generation?

Usually the source material Chaucer borrowed for his *Canterbury Tales* is mentioned in some detail by the editors of modern publications. One example will perhaps show how Chaucer manipulated his source to suit his own work: *The Wife of Bath's Tale* emphasises the stereotypical picture of women as great chatterboxes. In the course of her tale she refers to the Latin writer Ovid's story of King Midas, who was punished by being given a pair of ass's ears – a shameful fact hidden from all but his barber. Eventually, Ovid says, the barber could keep this sensational secret no longer, and whispered it to the reeds by the river – with predictable results. But Chaucer alters the story: the Wife gives the betrayal to Midas' wife, who promises to tell no one:

> But natheless, hir thoughte that she dide,
> That she so longe sholde a conseil hide;
> Hir thoughte it swal so soore aboute hir herte
> That nedely som word hire moste asterte;
> And sith she dorste telle it to no man,
> Doun to a mareys faste by she ran –
> Til she cam there, hir herte was a-fire –
> And as a bitore bombleth in the mire,
> She leyde hir mouth unto the water doun:
> 'Biwreye me nat, thou water, with thy soun,'
> Quod she; 'to thee I telle it and namo;
> Myn housbonde hath longe asses eris two!
> Now is myn herte al hool, now is it oute.'
> *Nevertheless she thought she would die*
> *if she had to keep the secret for so long;*
> *she thought it would make her heart burst*
> *so that some word of it would be forced out of her;*

and since she could tell it to no one,
she ran down to a nearby marshland –
her heart burned within her until she reached it –
and just like a bittern booming in the fenlands
she put her mouth down to the water:
'Don't give me away with your murmuring, you waters,'
she said, "I tell you and no one else,
my husband has two long ass's ears!
Now my heart feels much better, now I've said that.'

▶ Clearly the above extract is intended as a joke against women, but is its tone unpleasant, or is it simply humorous? It is worth remembering that the Wife of Bath herself is supposedly speaking here.

Identifying the sources

Christian sources

The best known Bible stories would have been familiar to all Chaucer's contemporaries, whether they could read or not. They were told and re-told in play, song, painting and poetry, and visible in the wall paintings and sculptures of churches. Stories from the Bible, together with legends associated with Christian beliefs, provided much of the material for sermons, particularly parables, and the Bible provided an enormous amount of source material for the writings of fourteenth century writers. Both Langland in *Piers Plowman* and the writer of the Saddlers'play in the *York Mystery Plays* write vividly, for example, about the Harrowing of Hell – a theme developed from parts of the book of Isaiah and from the Psalms. Both use the story according to the apocryphal gospel of Nicodemus, which relates Christ's descent into Hell to save the souls of the righteous:

JESUS   *Atollite portas, principes,*
           Open up, ye princes of pain sere,
           Et elevamini eternales,
           Your endless gates that ye have here.
SATAN   What page is there that makes press
           And calls him king of us in fere?

(York Mystery Plays)

'Lift up your heads, O ye gates;' (Psalm 24:7)
Open up you princes of all manner of anguish,
'and be ye lift up, ye everlasting doors' (Psalm 24:7)
these everlasting gates that you have here.

What young knave is this, making this commotion
and calling himself king of all of us?

'Suffre we,'sayde Treuthe; 'I here and se bothe
A spirit speketh to Helle and bit to unspere the gates.'
Attollite portas.
A vois loude in that liht to Lucifer saide:
'*Princepes* of this place, prest undo this gates,
For here he cometh with croune, the kynge of all glorie!'
Thenne syhed Satoun and saide to Helle,
'Suche a lyht ayenes oure leve Lazar hit fette;
Care and combraunce is come to us alle.'

(Piers Plowman)

'Be quiet,' said Truth, 'I can hear and see
a spirit commands Hell to unlock the gates'.
'Lift your heads, O ye gates'.
A loud voice from within the light spoke to Lucifer:
'Princes of this place, open up the gates,
for here he comes crowned, the king of all glory!'
Then Satan sighed and said to Hell,
'Such light came to raise our dear Lazarus;
grief and distress has come to us all.'

▶ Such a dramatic (and reassuring) story was extremely popular in fourteenth century England. Why would it have been particularly attractive to these two writers? Do the two extracts have a different impact and emphasis?

Other Christian writings, such as the works of St. Augustine, St. Jerome and St. Paul, would also be familiar to many, because of the frequency with which they were mentioned in church, and the fact that often well-known passages from these writers were translated from Greek or Latin, and included in religious anthologies. Bible stories and references to the ideas of many Old and New Testament authorities provide themes and background for most of *The Canterbury Tales*.

Classical sources

Many popular stories from Greek and Roman legend and history were collected in anthologies, providing valuable source material for many writers, Chaucer included. Foremost amongst these was probably Ovid's *Metamorphoses*, entertaining accounts of the activities of classical deities, used extensively by Chaucer and, particularly, Gower. Chaucer also shows knowledge of the writings of Cato, Cicero, the historian Valerius Maximus, the philosophy of Theofrastus and tales from the *Aeneid* and the *Odyssey*. Although a voracious reader, Chaucer did not necessarily read any of these in their entirety (indeed, his information about the Trojan wars was lifted from Italian reworkings of classical material). His debt to the philosopher Boethius is more obvious, as can be seen below.

- Boethius (c. 475–525)
  A highly principled Roman consul, philosopher and writer, falsely imprisoned for treason, and ultimately executed, Boethius wrote *De Consolatione Philosophiae,* harmonising with Christian teaching. Chaucer repeatedly refers to his observation that humanity constantly complains about the unfairness of Fate, which seems to punish the good and reward the evil. This, Boethius asserted, is because we only see one small part of the pattern, and justice and harmony do triumph in the fullness of time. Boethian philosophy permeates works such as *Troilus and Criseyde* and *The Knight's Tale.* A lover, Arcite, in *The Knight's Tale,* longs for release from prison only to discover that this release, the thing he thought would bring him greatest happiness, will actually banish him from the sight of Emily, his beloved. Later, even when he seems to have succeeded in winning her hand in marriage, Fate delivers another deadly blow. Chaucer suggests that ardent searching for happiness can be mistaken, and his words echo Boethius' teaching very closely:

  > We faren as he that dronke is as a mous.
  > A dronke man woot wel he hath an hous,
  > But he noot which the righte wey is thider,
  > And to a dronke man the wey is slider.
  > And certes, in this world so faren we;
  > We seken faste after felicitee,
  > But we goon wrong ful often, trewely.

  > *We behave like a man who is drunk as a mouse* [very drunk].
  > *A drunk man knows very well he has a house*
  > *but can't work out how to get there*
  > *and the way to it is slippery and elusive to a drunkard,*
  > *and this is absolutely how we travel through life:*
  > *we rush eagerly after happiness*
  > *but we often get it absolutely wrong.*

▶ These words refer to one of the 'heroes' in the tale. What effect is achieved by indirectly likening him to someone 'as drunk as a mouse'?

Continental sources: French

The debt to French literature has already been mentioned. As a young poet at the English court, Chaucer's first impulse seems to have been to imitate and to translate these texts, concerned with Arthurian romances, love and chivalry. Magic also featured strongly in the early French songs and poems, and this too Chaucer incorporates into his own works, notably *The Franklin's Tale*.

- Chrétien de Troyes (1170–1190)
  He worked and wrote at the court of Marie de Champagne, daughter of Eleanor of Aquitaine. The French slant on the Arthurian romances is largely derived from the works of this writer, as are many of the elaborate conventions and attitudes of courtly love romances, found in Chaucer's writings, and also in those of Hoccleve, Lydgate and in *Sir Gawain and the Green Knight*.

- Marie de France
  A contemporary of de Troyes, she wrote twelve *lais* or short stories based on Celtic or Breton myths in Anglo-Norman dialect sometime between 1160 and 1190. Although apparently French, she seems to have enjoyed a literary career largely in England. Her short stories frequently dealt with magical deeds and aristocratic characters, and the Breton *lai* – a concise romantic tale, sung or spoken – became a style of short story-telling with many imitators, including Chaucer in his *Franklin's Tale:*

  > Thise olde gentil Britouns in hir dayes
  > Of diverse aventures maden layes,
  > Rimeyed in hir firste Briton tonge;
  > Whiche layes with hir instrumentz they songe,
  > Or elles redden hem for hir plesaunce,
  > And oon of hem have I in remembraunce,
  > Which I shal seyn with good wil as I kan.

  > *In the olden days these noble aristocratic Bretons*
  > *made lays or tales about various adventures,*
  > *rhymed in the ancient Breton language,*
  > *accompanying these lays or songs on musical instruments*
  > *or else they read them for their entertainment;*
  > *I have remembered one of these*
  > *which I shall relate as well as I can.*

▶ In fact, the story the Franklin goes on to tell comes from the Italian, Boccaccio, and was never a Breton *lai* at all. Why should a franklin wish to suggest his familiarity with a type of story that was old-fashioned by the 1380s, though indisputably 'gentil'?

- *Roman de la Rose*
  This was one of the most famous and most influential pieces of medieval literature. Two writers were involved: Guillaume de Lorris wrote a courtly love allegory

(*c.*1230) set in a walled garden where the narrator/lover searched for his love, symbolised by the rose. Jean de Meun later continued the allegorical search for the rose in the form of a dream, which discussed the philosophical and moral implications involved in the nature of love, as well as the courtly fantasy. de Meun's writing introduced a satirical element too: ironic commentary upon the church, society as a whole and particularly the behaviour of women. It was extremely popular amongst literate men and women, and some of it was translated by Chaucer from the French into English in the fourteenth century as *The Romaunt of the Rose*. Many writers, Chaucer included, adopted the framework of dream allegories, and the ideals of courtly love, as well as the satire, in their own works.

There are frequent indications of Chaucer's use of material from the *Roman*. The character of Alison, the Wife of Bath, has her roots in 'La Vieille' a caricature by Jean de Meun of an old lewd woman who has made her way through life by sexual barter. The descriptions of unhappy married life in the same text are taken from the same source. In *The Merchant's Tale* the *Roman* is mentioned by name:

> He made a gardyn, walled al with stoon;
> So fair a gardyn woot I nowher noon.
> For, out of doute, I verraily suppose
> That he that wroot the Romance of the Rose
> Ne koude of it the beautee wel devise;

> *He made a garden walled round with stone;*
> *I do not know of a fairer garden anywhere.*
> *For, without doubt, I truly believe*
> *that the man who wrote the Roman de la Rose*
> *could hardly describe its beauty;*

In the *Roman,* the garden provided the stage for elaborate displays of courtly love, a place for idealised courtship, all ritual, nothing physical. The lecherous old knight, January, in *The Merchant's Tale* has created a similar garden for his beautiful young wife, May. She is the exquisite fresh rose he keeps within the garden, revelling in his ownership of this beautiful prize. In fact, she outwits him and enjoys the garden with her own choice of sexual partner. The setting for 'courtly love' has become the background for sordid physical encounters in this bitter tale of marital relations.

Continental sources: Italian

Chaucer's debt to the great Italian writers of his own century was considerable; they added a new vitality and humanism to the by now slightly old fashioned *genre* of the French courtly love story-telling.

- Francesco Petrarch (1304–1374)
  A friend of Boccaccio, Petrarch is probably best known for his love sonnets to his mistress, Laura. Chaucer translated one of these, and used it in *Troilus and Criseyde*. *The Clerk's Tale,* of patient Griselda, is a close adaptation of Petrarch's modification of one of Boccaccio's stories.

- Giovanni Boccaccio (1313–1375)
  Chaucer borrowed heavily from Boccaccio's stories and structure. *Il Filostrato* was a major source for *Troilus and Criseyde*. Many of *The Canterbury Tales* are based on tales originally used in Boccaccio's *Decameron*. *The Franklin's Tale* contains many elements of the Italian's story of a lady whose noble husband decides she must, for honour's sake, keep a foolish promise. The folly of allowing strangers to stay the night provides a moral for one of the *Decameron* stories as well as for *The Reeve's Tale*. *The Knight's Tale,* in which two knights are rivals in love for the beautiful Emilia, is closely based on another of Boccaccio's works, the *Teseida*.

  Most important, perhaps, is the idea Chaucer borrowed from Boccaccio of a series of stories told by various people, compared and discussed by both a fictional company and the writer's actual audience. Boccaccio's refugees from plague-ridden Florence all came from similar wealthy backgrounds, and were young, pampered darlings of Florentine society. Their stories were therefore remarkably similar in tone and outlook. Chaucer took this framework, refining it, and presenting a group of characters from all walks of life, whose priorities and obsessions would vary considerably.

- Dante Alighieri (1265–1321)
  Dante was the inspiration for the next generation of his own countrymen, and also for Chaucer, who recognised Dante's extraordinary breadth of vision and linguistic virtuosity. Ideas and phrases in works such as *The Parlement of Fowles, Troilus and Criseyde, The Knight's Tale* and *The Prioress' Tale,* all come from Dante, as does the lecture on *gentillesse* in *The Wife of Bath's Tale*. One of the bleakest stories in *The Monk's Tale* is lifted directly from Dante's *Inferno* – the tale of Ugolino, Count of Pisa, who died of starvation, along with his three young sons:

  > Thus ended is this myghty Erl of Pize.
  > From heigh estaat Fortune awey hym carf.
  > Of this tragedie it oghte ynough suffise;
  > Whoso wol here it in a lenger wise,
  > Redeth the grete poete of Ytaille
  > That highte Dant, for he kan al devyse
  > Fro point to point, nat o word wol he faille.

So ended the mighty Earl of Pisa.
Fortune cut him down from his high estate.
This should be sufficient detail of such a tragedy;
should anyone wish to learn more detail
he should read the great Italian poet
called Dante, for he can tell it all
from beginning to end, without leaving out anything.

But the most important gift Dante bequeathed to Chaucer was to show him that commonplace, everyday language, whether it be Italian or English, could be forged into great poetry to rival that of the classical masters.

Using the sources

Treatises and educational texts

Then, as now, writers wanted to inform, persuade and divert their audience; the best also sought to create something artistically admirable. The purpose for which each text was written would usually affect the style of its writing. Mandeville's *Travels,* for instance, began as a helpful guide book for medieval tourists, but it was also read as a book of entertainment. Whilst Julian of Norwich and other mystics of the fourteenth century wanted readers to grasp the essence of spiritual awareness, writers of grammar primers, or instruction manuals for scholars at schools and universities, would have very different aims. Chaucer himself produced an instruction manual on the astrolabe (an essential astronomical instrument) in 1491, dedicated to his son, Lewis:

> Lyte Lowys my sone, I aperceyve wel by certeyne evydences thyn abilite to lerne sciences touching nombres and proporciouns *[numbers and angles]*; and as wel considre I thy besy praier *[anxious request]* in special to lerne the tretys *[functions]* of the Astrelabie.

This treatise reveals two things: Chaucer's own fascination and certain expertise in astronomy, and his nature as a loving and interested father. Lewis could not have been very old, for his father simplifies the treatise, on the grounds that some aspects of the use of an astrolabe 'ben to harde to thy tendir age to conceyve'.

Literary texts

The following categories of literature can all be found in *The Canterbury Tales,* and other contemporary texts:

- Courtly love romances
  Deriving from the French tradition, these sometimes take the form of songs or ballads. Often they are concerned with high moral issues, and idealistic, heroic attitudes. *Sir Gawain and the Green Knight* belongs to this tradition, and Chaucer also uses it in his earliest works, such as the *Boke of the Duchess,* in *Troilus and Criseyde* and in many of his *Canterbury Tales,* notably the tales told by the Knight, the Squire, the Franklin, and Chaucer's own interrupted *Tale of Sir Thopas.*

- *Fabliaux*
  These are more worldly, vulgar and comical stories, usually about the exploits of common people, rather than aristocrats, and often involve knockabout humour. Although Chaucer protests in *The Canterbury Tales* that such stories, told by his low-class pilgrims, will offend the delicate sensibilities of others, they were enjoyed by all levels of society. Boccaccio included them in his *Decameron* and similar stories appeared in French and Flemish literature. Two of the best known *fabliaux* are *The Miller's Tale* and *The Reeve's Tale.*

▶ Although Chaucer is capable of combining humour, tragedy and pathos in all his stories, comedy was more usually associated with the antics of ordinary people in medieval literature. Is this still the case? Would you expect a different type of humour in writings about more aristocratic characters?

- Fables
  There are tales found in all world literature in which animals display the faults and weaknesses of human beings. Usually they contain a moral message. Chaucer would have known Aesop's fables, dating from the sixth century BC, and retold in most European languages. *The Nun's Priest's Tale* centres on one of many fables describing a cunning and resourceful fox. Other tales told by the pilgrims contain references to fables that were as popular then as now.

- Holy or moral tales
  Tales in which characters provide an inspiring illustration of exemplary behaviour abounded in fourteenth century literature, and were often incorporated in sermons as illustrations of a particular theme. *Troilus and Criseyde* contains elements of the extended moral treatise. *The Clerk's Tale* of patient Griselda suggests that virtue and meekness in a wife will finally be rewarded. *The Physician's Tale* is about Virginia – a girl so virtuous she accepts death rather than dishonour. *The Prioress' Tale* is a sentimental tale of a little seven-year old 'clergeon' – a small pupil at a clerks' school – whose murdered body, thrown on a dungheap, continues to sing praises to the Virgin after death. *The Monk's Tale* is a series of edifying examples of famous people, which becomes so tedious that even the courteous Knight begs him to stop – a 'litel hevynesse' is enough for most people; the Monk has given them a bucketful. The Host's criticism is blunter:

Sire Monk, namoore of this, so God yow blesse!
Youre tale anoyeth al this compaignie.
Swich talking is nat worth a boterflye,
For therinne is ther no desport ne game.
Wherfore, sire Monk, or daun Piers by youre name,
I pray yow hertely telle us somwhat elles;

Sir Monk, no more of this, God bless you!
your story is boring everyone.
Such talk is worthless [not worth a butterfly],
for there's no entertainment or fun in it.
And so, sir Monk, or Sir Peter, to call you by name,
I heartily beg you to tell us something else;

- Sermons
  These were often the only entertainment available to poor people in isolated
  country areas. They usually focused on one particular vice – Avarice, Envy, Wrath –
  illustrated by a Biblical text and stories from the Bible or familiar literature.
  Chaucer makes it clear in the Prologue to *The Pardoner's Tale* that a sermon was
  often a dramatic *tour de force,* intended to squeeze generous donations from the
  audience. The Monk would obviously have fared badly in such circumstances: his
  story-telling skills are limited; but the Pardoner boasts of his success:

Thanne telle I hem ensamples many oon
Of olde stories longe time agoon.
For lewed peple loven tales olde;
Swiche thinges kan they wel reporte and holde.
What, trowe ye that whiles I may preche,
And winne gold and silver for I teche,
That I wol live in poverte wilfully?

Then I tell them many moral tales
taken from old stories of long ago,
for simple folk love old stories,
they can remember and repeat such tales.
Well, do you really think that while I can preach
and gain plenty of gold and silver for my teaching
that I would really choose to live a life of poverty?

The Parson's Tale also takes the form of a sermon, or moral treatise, but its impact
and its significance differ widely from the flashy achievement of the acquisitive
Pardoner. The last tale in the series, as the pilgrims are approaching Canterbury,

falls to the Parson, and the Host speaks for all when he asks this sincere, deeply religious man to give them something worthwhile. The Parson promises no fables, no flattery, no embroidery – just the unadulterated truth. His prologue indicates the purpose of his sermon:

> And Jhesu, for his grace, wit me sende
> To shewe yow the wey, in this viage,
> Of thilke parfit glorious pilgrymage
> That highte Jerusalem celestial.

> *And Jesus, in his love and grace, will give me the ability*
> *to show you, during our travels, the way*
> *to make the perfect and glorious pilgrimage*
> *to that place called heavenly Jerusalem.*

▶ The contrast between the aims and attitudes of these two preachers is clear from the quotations above. How does Chaucer emphasise this through both the style and content of the quotations above?

- Confessions
  The issue of confession may be found in Chaucer's *Boke of the Duchess,* and recurs frequently throughout *The Canterbury Tales*. Almost all Chaucer's characters reveal their weaknesses and mistakes to the audience, deliberately or by accident. *The Canon's Yeoman's Prologue* and *Tale* is the confession of a runaway servant who reveals every trick involved in the art of pretending to turn base metal into gold, as practised by his former master, a fanatical alchemist. *The Wife of Bath's Prologue* is a detailed account of her entrapment and domination of her five husbands; *The Franklin's Prologue* confesses his wish that his reprobate son will become a gentleman like the Squire; the Pardoner confesses how he extracts money from his congregations. Chaucer also allows his characters to reveal more than they realise. We can tell that the Franklin longs to acquire the veneer of *gentillesse* he admires in the Knight and his son; that the Wife yearns for happiness from husband number six (wherever he may be), but never realises that her behaviour makes such happiness impossible; that the Pardoner, supposedly the person who can bring ordinary people to an awareness of spiritual salvation, has no understanding of spiritual values at all; that the Merchant cordially dislikes his wife, the Reeve is bitter and lonely – and so on.

Using the literary genres

Chaucer frequently parodies and satirises courtly love ideals. The knight who figures in *The Wife of Bath's Tale* cuts a sorry figure: first seen riding along beside the river (a traditional introduction to a romantic hero), he rapes the first maiden he meets, rather than saving her from such a fate, and is ultimately forced to marry a cunning, low class, old woman. The knight in *The Merchant's Tale*, grasping, lecherous January, is duped by May, his lovely young bride, whose fair face hides a coldly calculating nature. The honourable code of conduct, so much a part of the courtly love tradition, is torn to shreds when May and the knight's 'faithful' squire have sex in January's perfect garden.

The Franklin's Tale presents a noble lady who, faced with a fearful dilemma, turns to the traditional rhetorical device of lamenting against cruel Fate. Her excessively long lament is a parody of the genre, and becomes ridiculous (but lasts long enough for her husband to return home, thus avoiding the need for suicide).

The Tale of Sir Thopas, that Chaucer, the pilgrim, gives to himself to tell, is an atrocious parody of contemporary 'romances'. Chaucer takes the themes associated with knightly behaviour – riding out in search of adventure, encounters with giants, elf-queens, feasting – and turns them into something comical in its dreadfulness. Poor Sir Thopas is an unlikely hero. The tale abounds with anti-climax and cliché. Verse form and language emphasise its absurdities and inadequacies:

> Til that ther cam a greet geaunt,
> His name was sire Olefaunt,
> A perilous man of dede.
> He seyde, 'Child, by Termagaunt!
> But if thou prike out of myn haunt,
> Anon I sle thy steede
> With mace.
> Heere is the queene of Fayerye,
> With harpe and pipe and symphonye,
> Dwellynge in this place.'

> *Till along came a huge giant,*
> *His name was Sir Elephant,*
> *a dangerous man indeed.*
> *He said 'Childe* [as in Childe Harold] *by Termagent* [imaginary god]!
> *unless you leave my homeground*
> *I shall immediately kill your horse*
> *With my club.*
> *The queen of the fairies*
> *lives here,*
> *with harp, pipe and symphony.*

His fellow travellers beg Chaucer to stop, as the courtly romance moves turgidly onwards, and dwindles to a halt. It is Chaucer's joke against himself.

Chaucer mixes up the genres, so that no tale can be read as 'simply' one thing or another. *The Nun's Priest's Tale,* for example, is a splendidly told fable; it is also a sermon on the folly of vanity and as well a parody of courtly behaviour, for here, as in *The Parlement of Fowles,* birds behave and speak like nobility.

▶ The passage on page 86, Part 3, is a description of a cockerel in mock-heroic form; what does Chaucer achieve by this juxtaposition of barnyard and lordly appearance? Compare the passage with the anonymous description of a cockerel on page 96.

Two notable parodies appear early in the *Tales;* the Knight has told a romantic story of Palamon and Arcite, in love with the beautiful and inaccessible Emily. This is followed first by *The Miller's Tale,* in which an attractive young wife is loved by two young men of the town: Absalon, a foppish, foolish parish clerk, and a smooth-talking young scholar 'hende Nicholas'. By contrast with *The Knight's Tale,* this 'heroine' is 'wylde and yonge', quite prepared to cheat her old husband. The love triangle in *The Miller's Tale* becomes the subject of a cruelly comical and cheerfully amoral story.

The Reeve's Tale also parodies ideals of courtly love. Malyne, a cheating miller's daughter, is described as having some of the characteristics of a typical courtly heroine – eyes 'grey as glass', high breasts, long, beautiful hair – but these are cruelly combined with other features that emphasise her common origins – broad hips and snub nose. Although she weeps in a manner that imitates the actions of a courtly heroine when her lover rides away, their relationship has been no more than a swift sexual encounter, with no affection. And, rather than offering her hero the traditional magic sword or similar courtly gift beloved by the romantic writers, Malyne sends him on his way with a large loaf:

> 'Now, deere lemman,' quod she, 'go, far weel!
> But er thow go, o thing I wol thee telle:
> Whan that thou wendest homward by the melle,
> Right at the entree of the dore bihinde
> Thou shalt a cake of half a busshel finde
> That was ymaked of thyn owene mele,
> Which that I heelp my sire for to stele.
> And, goode lemman, God thee save and kepe!'
> And with that word almoost she gan to wepe.

> *'Now, my beloved,' she said, 'be gone! fare well!*
> *but before you go I'll tell you one thing:*
> *as you turn for home beside the mill*
> *right by the entrance to the back door*

you'll find a half-bushel loaf
made from your own grain,
which I helped my father steal.
And, dear lover, God save and keep you safe!'
And with those words she almost burst out crying.

The Clerk's Tale, about the superhuman patience and meekness of silent Griselda, contains elements of folklore. It can be read as a moral lesson, celebrating the virtues of forbearance and stoicism, and condemning the cruel behaviour of the Count. Some critics see a Christ-like sacrifice in the behaviour of Griselda. It can also be seen as the antithesis of *The Wife of Bath's Tale,* told by that most garrulous of Chaucer's travellers. Both tales then become part of a 'marriage debate' about the role of women in society, a debate that popularly encompasses two other tales in particular, *The Franklin's Tale* and *The Merchant's Tale.*

The Canterbury Tales

Comparison with other contemporary works

Collections of short stories were common and popular in the fourteenth century; usually these collections were moral in tone, and all told in a similar manner. The idea of story-telling competitions was also familiar to Chaucer's original audience, since story-telling was a popular social pastime. Many medieval writers wrote 'estates satire', in which all members of contemporary society, from the highest to the lowest, were described, and their faults vigorously criticised. The *Tales* are made up of romances, *fabliaux*, treatises, sermons, moral fables – all of which can be found in other texts of the fourteenth century.

So why is Chaucer's story collection so special? One distinguishing innovation is the combination of a survey of society, an 'estates satire', with a collection of stories. By using the framework of a group of pilgrims, he is able to include a wide swathe of social types among his story-tellers. The detailed description of each of them before the tales begin allows him to use the character of each teller, thus established, to illuminate the tale and the attitude of the teller to his or her subject matter. The tone is set by Chaucer's insistence that it is all a game – a ploy which excuses him from taking a moral stance on what is being said. Readers are invited to judge for themselves, and also to see how the moral slant in each story is often influenced by the self-interest of the teller. By making Harry Bailly Master of Ceremonies and judge of the story-telling, Chaucer invites not just the fictional audience, but us, the listening and reading audience, to 'judge' whatever the pilgrims say, taking into account what Chaucer tells us about them (and what he allows them to tell about themselves).

▶ Look at one or two tales that you know. How far does the character Chaucer gives to the teller influence what is being told? The extract from *The Prioress' Tale* on page 85 may be useful here.

The General Prologue

The way in which Chaucer describes his group differs subtly from that of most contemporary satirists. There is no apparent anger in his tone; often he seems not to be satirising at all. By adopting the role of a guileless fellow pilgrim, Chaucer allows the judgement of each character described to appear to come from us, rather than him. Here again, the audience is invited to take an active role in the entertainment.

The short account of the guildsmen's Cook is presented without any apparent attempt to judge him. How, then, does Chaucer provoke our response to him?

A Cook they hadde with hem for the nones
To boille the chiknes with the marybones,
And poudre-marchant tart and galingale.
Wel koude he knowe a draughte of Londoun ale.
He koude rooste, and sethe, and broille, and frie,
Maken mortreux, and wel bake a pie.
But greet harm was it, as it thoughte me,
That on his shine a mormal hadde he.
For blankmanger, that made he with the beste.

They had a Cook with them for this occasion
to boil the chickens with marrowbones,
with sharp flavourings and spices.
He could easily identify a jar of London ale.
He could roast, simmer, boil and fry,
make thick soups and bake pies.
But I thought it was quite a pity
that he had a running sore on his leg.
He was one of the best at making blancmange.

How the *Tales* begin

Although near the end of *The General Prologue* Chaucer apologises for not having 'set folk in hir degree', he has taken some care to place first in his *Prologue* those highest up the social scale – the Knight and his son (with their servant) and the Prioress. He ends with a couple of objectionable and distinctly shady customers – the Pardoner and the Summoner. The Host is certainly aware of social distinctions; his comments to individual members of the group are quite a good guide to their social status. Chaucer himself seems to be addressed with a sort of good-natured contempt. When fate decrees that the Knight should tell the first tale, all seem to feel this is appropriate, and we may well expect the rest of the stories will be told in predictable sequence. Social order is being politely maintained, and Chaucer underlines this by the way *The Knight's Tale* is received:

> Whan that the Knight had thus his tale ytoold,
> In al the route nas ther yong ne oold
> That he ne seide it was a noble storie,
> And worthy for to drawen to memorie;
> And namely the gentils everichon.

> *When the knight had told his tale*
> *no member of the group, young or old,*
> *could deny that this was a fine, noble story,*
> *well worth remembering;*
> *most particularly all the upper class pilgrims.*

Although the Monk is invited to hold forth next, something much more interesting occurs. The drunken Miller demands to speak, and the Host cannot silence him, eventually giving up and disclaiming all responsibility for what happens next. The careful fabric of social status is torn away, and the voices of common people, the Miller, the Reeve and the Cook, demand to be heard. It is no accident that Chaucer's group is making a journey which mirrors that other journey, made in 1381, when peasants, marching from Canterbury to London, led by Wat Tyler, demanded that their voices should be heard by the king. The suggestion of anarchy, which Chaucer allows to intrude into his *Tales,* adds an important element to the work. Chaucer, like the Host, refuses to be held responsible for what his characters say.

Links between tales

Even though scholars are unable to decide absolutely the order in which the tales should be presented, it is possible to see that some clearly follow others. The fragment of manuscript containing *The Miller's Tale,* for example, shows that it follows *The Knight's Tale,* and is itself followed by that of the Reeve. There are several links between these three. First, Miller and Reeve both tell *fabliaux* which parody the romantic element of *The Knight's Tale.* Second, the Miller's cheerfully vulgar account of the unfortunate affairs of an old and gullible carpenter is taken as a personal insult by the Reeve, himself both old and a carpenter by trade. His own story about a cheating miller satisfies him that 'Thus have I quyt the Miller in my tale'.

Other tales and tellers have clear links between them: the Wife of Bath, angry that the Friar laughs at her long-winded *Prologue,* retaliates by introducing the idea of lecherous friars early in her story. Again, *The Friar's Tale* (about a summoner who happily keeps company with the Devil) is followed, predictably, by *The Summoner's Tale* about a smooth-talking friar who wheedles himself into the favours of a rich man and his attractive wife, both of whom welcome him warmly into their home:

> 'Now, maister,'quod the wyf, 'er that I go,
> What wol ye dyne? I wol go theraboute.'
> 'Now dame,'quod he,' now, *je vous dy sanz doute,*
> Have I nat of a capon but the lyvere,
> And of youre softe breed nat but a shyvere,
> And after that a rosted pigges heed —
> But that I nolde no beest for me were deed —
> Thanne hadde I with yow hoomly suffisaunce.
> I am a man of litel sustenaunce;
> My spirit hath his fostryng in the Bible.

> *'Now sir,' said the wife, 'before I go*
> *what do you fancy for supper? I'll go and prepare it.'*
> *'Now my lady,' he said, 'now I tell you truly,*
> *I'll have just the liver of a capon*
> *with just a sliver of your soft, white bread*
> *and after that a roast pig's head —*
> *but don't trouble yourself to kill one just for me —*
> *then I'll have had a simple satisfying meal with you.*
> *I'm a man who needs little food:*
> *my spirit is nourished by the Bible.*

▶ What information does Chaucer convey about both wife and friar from this short conversation?

The tales of the Clerk, the Wife of Bath, the Merchant and the Franklin may be discussed as a group offering widely differing views on marital relationships. Though Chaucer raises many questions on the subject, he provides no definitive answers. He returns again and again to the question of harmony in relationships between men and women, but never offers a recipe for an ideal relationship. The Wife might think that women require:

> Housbondes meeke, yonge, and fressh abedde,
> And grace t'overbide hem that we wedde;

but not many readers or listeners to her tale would imagine she offers the right answer to marital problems. The Franklin begins his tale with an apparent recipe for perfect domestic harmony, in which husband and wife promise one another equal partnership, the knight promising he will continue to be his lady's 'servant in love' whilst also being her 'lord in marriage'. Domestic harmony certainly prevails for the first two years, but the wife's freedom of speech leads to disaster, only prevented when she restores to her husband his conventional role of lord and master.

The role of the author

As the fictional journey towards Canterbury begins, Chaucer reminds his audience that the story-telling contest is a game, and that the characters assembled are both passive listeners and active participants in the process. Chaucer's own stance on the issues he raises is hidden within a complex creation of masks and disguises. Even the tale being told is hardly handled straightforwardly. Frequently the main 'plot' is almost lost in a maze of sub-plots and digressions that can exasperate a reader who prefers everything to be cut and dried. Chaucer the invisible, and apparently passive, creator is in fact building up a collection of ideas and considerations with which to colour the response of his audience.

▶ Consider any one of Chaucer's *Tales* that you know well. Does it have any digressions from the main plot? What do they add to the tale?

Just as the audience is invited to consider a straightforward narrative from various standpoints, so too Chaucer often requires us to re-assess attitudes to particular characters. Most notably in his earlier work *Troilus and Criseyde,* he makes Criseyde a rounded and sympathetic character, even though his source material tended to brand her as a stereotype of an untrustworthy woman, the byword for infidelity down the centuries. January, in *The Merchant's Tale,* is another case in point. The initial portrait of him is unsympathetic: hunting for a young wife, like some particularly attractive bargain in the market, rushing through the wedding ceremony to get her into bed, and exulting in his prize like the revolting old lecher he clearly is, he can only provoke disgust in his audience. But when it becomes clear that 'fresshe May' is as grasping and unscrupulous as her husband, prepared to trick him and betray him without a qualm, our sympathies may stray from the wife towards the blind and gullible husband.

Even our attitude towards narrators can alter: *The Knight's Tale* is a splendid example of a romance embodying all chivalrous aspects of love and war, and it is told by that noble example of chivalry, the 'verray parfit, gentil knyght'. As it progresses, the fundamental issues – that both love and war are honourable, noble pursuits – are subjected to careful, critical examination. Is the noble Knight justified in celebrating this world of war and chivalry? Is the love for Emily that so decisively destroys the friendship between Palamon and Arcite romantic and wonderful or foolishly damaging? Again, as the Wife of Bath relates both her *Prologue* and her *Tale,* should the audience deplore her monstrous egotism, applaud her fighting spirit, or pity her lack of awareness of what love might really be? And as the boastful Pardoner finishes his powerful warning against the sin of avarice by collecting as much financial benefit as he can, do we loathe him for his lack of conscience or pity him for his spiritual blindness? Or both?

▶ Choose two characters from *The General Prologue* or any of the *Tales* and decide how Chaucer creates an ambivalent response to them. You could use the description of Alison from *The Miller's Tale* on page 91.

How the *Tales* finish

Chaucer may have intended to add more tales to his work, but it seems possible that the idea of an arrival in Canterbury was never part of his final design. The ending is structured to present the light-hearted story-telling competition from a different perspective. As evening falls, and the end of the pilgrimage seems imminent, the mood alters. The Host turns to the Parson to have the final say. The Parson is in no mood for games; his dedication to the business of saving souls is as clear here as it was in *The General Prologue:*

> Thou getest fable noon ytoold for me;
> For Paul, that writeth unto Thymothee,
> Repreveth hem that weyven soothfastnesse,
> And tellen fables and swich wrecchednesse.
> Why sholde I sowen draf out of my fest,
> When I may sowen whete, if that me lest?

> *You will get no story-telling as far as I'm concerned;*
> *For Paul, writing to Timothy*
> *rebukes those who set aside plain truthfulness,*
> *and tell stories and similar folly.*
> *Why should I let chaff dribble out of my hand*
> *when I am able to sow good wheat if I choose?*

What follows is a hard-hitting, authoritative analysis of penitence – recognising and regretting one's sin (the act of contrition), confessing to a priest and to God and receiving the satisfaction of making amends and gaining forgiveness. It has already been seen that the Bible has provided much source material in earlier tales. The Wife of Bath, the Pardoner and the Monk all use the Scriptures for their own ends. The Parson uses the Bible to save souls, thus remaining totally true to his calling:

To drawen folk to hevene by fairnesse
By good ensample, this was his bisynesse.

Some critics believe *The Parson's Tale* was a late addition to *The Canterbury Tales,* since it presents such a devastatingly serious ending to the light-hearted 'game' that began on that April morning. If a parallel may be drawn between an actual pilgrimage to Canterbury and the human journey through life towards a spiritual goal, then it seems fitting that the 'game' becomes more thoughtful and serious as it nears completion.

The final passage of the *Tales* is headed 'Heere taketh the makere of this book his leve' (see Part 3, page 92). Chaucer the man at last seems to step forward, abandoning the mask of Chaucer the bumbling, good-natured and inept pilgrim, to make his own confession along the lines suggested by *The Parson's Tale*. The last voice we hear is the author's, listing his writings, asking forgiveness for having written about some frivolous matters, but also thanking God for giving him the grace to write others. He offers some justification for even his most worldly writings.

▶ Chaucer's *Retractions* reveal the writer in a very different light. Is this the 'real' Chaucer? Such disclaimers by medieval authors were relatively common. How appropriate is such a conclusion? Does it downgrade what came before, or is it just another part of the patchwork of human experience that makes up *The Canterbury Tales* as they survive today?

Assignments

1   Do you believe that only by reading medieval texts in the original language it is possible to appreciate them to the full? Compare any passage you know well with a modern translation. What has been gained, or lost, in the translation?

2   Why might it be said that English literature of the fourteenth century was essentially European in a way that is not true of 'English' literature today?

3   How does the content and style of Chaucer's writing seem to compare with what you have seen of the works of his contemporaries to be found in this book?

4   If so much of Chaucer's material came from other sources, can he really be admired as a creative writer?

5 What we have of *The Canterbury Tales* is fragmentary. We cannot be certain that all the tales have survived, nor can we be sure of the order in which Chaucer intended them to be presented. Does this matter?

6 Chaucer's pilgrims never reach Canterbury. The issues they discuss, about society, relationships, religion, are never resolved. What effect does this have on your response to *The Canterbury Tales?*

7 *The Canterbury Tales* invite us to question attitudes and ideas, and suggest that most points of view are coloured by the speaker's personality. Does this detract from or add to their interest? Choose one or two tales you know well to illustrate your argument.

8 The rhyming couplet, used so often in *The Canterbury Tales,* is extremely versatile. By close study of two or three passages from Part 3, discuss the different effects achieved using this style.

9 If you were a fourteenth century writer, wishing to satirise or criticise some aspect of contemporary life, what subject(s) might you choose for your satire? What methods would you choose to employ? How would you set about it?

10 Using two or more of the extracts from Part 3, compare the most significant differences of vocabulary, grammar and style between fourteenth century and contemporary writing.

3 | Texts and extracts

The extracts included in this section have been chosen to illustrate key themes and aspects of style and language mentioned elsewhere in the book. They should provide material useful when working on tasks and assignments to be found in other sections. Unless otherwise stated, the passages are by Chaucer, though not necessarily from *The Canterbury Tales*.

Geoffrey Chaucer

From *The Pardoner's Tale*

The Pardoner has finished his account of the three murderous thieves, each of whom dies violently whilst attempting to keep stolen gold for himself alone. Moving seamlessly from the conclusion of his tale to a general warning about sin, the Pardoner urges his audience to repent, before it is too late.

O 'cursed sinne of alle cursednesse!	*most accursed sin*
O 'traitours homicide, O wikkednesse!	*treacherous murder*
O glotonye, 'luxurie, and hasardrye!	*lechery and gambling*
Thou 'blasphemour of Crist with vileynye	*who use Christ's name blasphemously*
And 'othes grete, of ''usage and of pride!	*oaths, habit*
Allas! mankinde, 'how may it bitide	*how has it happened*
That to thy creatour, 'which that the wroghte,	*who made you*
And with his precious herte-blood 'thee boghte,	*bought you*
Thou art so fals and so unkinde, allas?	
Now, goode men, God 'foryeve yow youre trespas,	*forgive*
And 'ware yow fro the sinne of avarice!	*be careful to avoid*
Myn hooly pardoun may yow alle 'warice,	*cure*
'So that ye offre ''nobles or sterlinges,	*as long as, silver coins*
Or elles silver broches, spoones, ringes.	
Boweth youre heed under this 'hooly bulle!	*holy [and official] licence*
Cometh up, ye wives, offreth of youre 'wolle!	*wool*
Youre names I entre heer 'in my rolle anon;	*on my list immediately*
Into the blisse of hevene shul ye gon.	
I yow 'assoille by myn heigh power,	*pardon*
'Yow that wol offre,	*those of you who will make an offering*

From *Troilus and Criseyde,* Book V

Criseyde has become a political pawn in negotiations between Greeks and Trojans. Although she had pledged her love to Troilus, she has now succumbed to the Greek, Diomed. Troilus still hopes that she will return to him, but she seems to believe her surrender to Diomed is inevitable.

But trewely, the storie telleth us,	
Ther 'made nevere womman moore wo	no woman ever lamented more
Than she, whan that she 'falsed Troilus.	betrayed
She seyde, 'Allas, for now is 'clene ago	completely destroyed
My 'name of trouthe in love, for everemo!	reputation
For I have falsed 'oon the gentileste	one of the most noble
That evere was, and oon the worthieste!	
Allas, of me, unto the worldes ende,	
Shal neyther ben ywriten nor ysonge	
No good word, for thise bokes wol me 'shende.	will destroy me
O, 'rolled shal I ben on many a tonge!	my name will be rolled on many a tongue!
Thoroughout the world 'my belle shal be ronge!	my name will ring out
And wommen moost wol haten me of alle.	
Allas, that 'swich a cas me sholde falle!	such a fate
Thei wol seyn, 'in as muche as in me is,	through what is in my nature,
'I have hem don deshonour, weylaway!	I have dishonoured them too
'Al be I nat the first that dide amys,	though I'm not the first woman to do wrong
What helpeth that to 'don my blame awey?	excuse my guilt
But 'syn I se ther is no bettre way	since
And that to late is now for me to 'rewe,	regret what's happened
To Diomede 'algate I wol be trewe.	at least

From *The Wife of Bath's Prologue*

The Wife tells her audience about life with her first three husbands, all of whom were old men she married for money. Here she reveals how she kept each one under control.

For winning wolde I 'al his lust endure,	put up with all his passion
And make me a 'feyned appetit;	pretended to enjoy it
And yet 'in bacon hadde I nevere delit;	I'd never enjoyed old flesh
That made me that 'evere I wolde hem chide.	nag him constantly
For 'thogh the pope hadde seten hem biside,	even if the pope had been sitting beside him

I wolde nat spare hem 'at hir owene bord;	*at his own table;*
For, by my trouthe, 'I quitte hem word for word.	*I got the better of him*
As helpe me 'verray God omnipotent,	*all-powerful God*
Though I right now 'sholde make my testament,	*had to make my dying testament*
I 'ne owe hem nat a word that it nis quit.	*There's not one word that hasn't been paid back*
I 'broghte it so aboute by my wit	*arranged things in such a way*
That they moste 'yeve it up, as for the beste,	*surrender*
Or elles hadde we 'nevere been in reste.	*never have stopped fighting*
For thogh he looked as a 'wood leon,	*mad lion*
Yet 'sholde he faille of his conclusion.	*he would be unable to win his argument*
Thanne wolde I seye, "Goode lief, taak keep	*now, sweetie, just think*
'How mekely looketh Wilkin, oure sheep!	*how tame our old ram, Wilkin, looks*
Com neer, my spouse, lat me 'ba thy cheke!	*kiss your cheek*
Ye sholde been al pacient and 'meke,	*docile*
And 'han a sweete spiced conscience,	*be anxious to do what's right*
'Sith ye so preche of Jobes pacience.	*since*
'Suffreth alwey, sin ye so wel kan preche;	*always be patient*
And 'but ye do, certein we shal yow teche	*unless you are, we [women] will teach you*
That it is fair to 'have a wyf in pees.	*be at peace with your wife*
Oon of us two moste 'bowen, doutelees;	*give in*
And 'sith a man is moore resonable	*since*
Than womman is, 'ye moste been suffrable.	*you must learn to put up with things*

From *The Knight's Tale*

The Knight's Tale is largely concerned with the playing out of courtly love conventions, frequently emphasising how these clash with reality. Two noble young knights, imprisoned by Lord Theseus after the battle for Thebes, see from their prison cell the beautiful Emily, singing in her rose garden, one splendid May morning. They immediately fall in love with her, reacting according to the laws of romantic love. They have never seen her before; she does not see them. Nevertheless they squabble about who loved her first.

For 'paramour I loved hire first er thow.	*I loved her as a flesh and blood woman before you did*
What 'wiltow seyen? Thou ''woost nat yet now	*can you say to that? don't yet know*
Wheither she be a womman or goddesse!	
Thyn is 'affeccioun of hoolinesse,	*like a holy feeling,*
And myn is love, 'as to a creature;	*as to a living woman*
For which I tolde thee myn 'aventure	*situation*
As to my 'cosin and my brother sworn.	*cousin*

'I pose that thow lovedest hire biforn;	*I grant that you loved her first*
'Wostow nat wel the olde clerkes ''sawe,	*don't you know, old saying*
That ''who shal yeve a lovere any lawe?'	*law doesn't apply to a lover*
Love is a gretter lawe, 'by my pan,	*my head tells me*
Than may be yeve to any 'erthely man;	*earthly system of rights*
And therfore 'positif lawe and swich decree	*laws of possession*
Is broken al day for love 'in ech degree.	*in every way*
A man moot nedes love, 'maugree his heed.	*in spite of himself*
He 'may nat fleen it thogh he sholde be ''deed,	*can't escape it, dies*
'Al be she maide, or widwe, or elles wyf.	*whether*
And 'eek it is nat likly ''al thy lyf	*furthermore, ever in your life*
To 'stonden in hir grace; ''namoore shal I;	*find favour with her, nor shall I*
For wel thou woost thyselven, verraily,	
That thou and I be 'dampned to prisoun	*condemned*
Perpetuelly; us 'gaineth no raunsoun.	*get no ransom*
We strive as dide 'the houndes for the boon;	*dogs after a bone*
They foughte al day, and yet 'hir part was noon.	*got none of it*
Ther cam a kite, whil that they were 'so wrothe,	*in their furious state*
And baar awey the boon 'bitwixe hem bothe.	*from both of them*

From *The Merchant's Tale*

Like Emily, in *The Knight's Tale,* heroines in romances were customarily beautiful, and the phrase 'as fresh as the month of May' was a commonplace description of such girls. Sometimes the beauty hid less pleasant aspects, as in *The Merchant's Tale,* which tells of a knight who chooses his wife purely for her looks, and whose assessment of her character is based solely upon what he sees. Like a man setting up a mirror in a market-place, he looks over the various women from whom he might choose.

But nathelees, 'bitwixe ernest and game,	*half serious, half joking*
He atte last 'apointed him on oon,	*decided upon one*
And 'leet alle othere from his herte goon,	*banished the rest from his heart*
And chees hire 'of his owene auctoritee;	*on his own authority [took no advice]*
For love is blind 'alday, and may nat see.	*always*
And whan that he was in his bed ybroght,	
He 'purtreyed in his herte and in his thoght	*pictured in his heart and imagination*
Hir fresshe beautee and hir age tendre,	
Hir 'middel smal, hire armes longe and sklendre,	*her tiny waist*
Hir 'wise governaunce, hir gentillesse,	*her composed bearing, her noble nature*
Hir 'wommanly beringe, and hire ''sadnesse.	*womanly conduct, serious nature*
And whan that he 'on hire was condescended,	*he had decided on her*
Him thoughte 'his choys mighte nat ben amended.	*his choice could not be bettered*

From *The Prioress' Tale*

The Prioress' Tale concerns a little scholar, only child of a widowed mother, who sings an Advent anthem with simple religious fervour until murdered by wicked Jews, as he walks through the Jewish quarter on his way home. Such unthinking racial prejudice was not uncommon in the fourteenth century; Jewish communities had been tolerated, for the essential loans they made to the crown, but had been expelled from England in 1290. Stories of miracles were extremely popular in fourteenth century literature. Here the boy's mother searches for him everywhere – and a miracle occurs.

This poure widwe awaiteth al that night
After hir litel child, but he cam noght;
'For which, as soone as it was dayes light,   *and so*
With face pale of drede and 'bisy thoght,   *anguished thoughts*
She hath at scole and elleswhere him soght,
Til 'finally she gan so fer espie   *at last she found out*
That he last seyn was in the 'Juerie.   *Jewish area*

'With moodres pitee in hir brest enclosed,   *her heart full of a mother's anguish*
She gooth, as she were half out of hir minde,
To every place 'where she hath supposed   *where she imagined*
By liklihede hir litel child to finde;
And evere on Cristes mooder meeke and kinde
She cride, and atte laste thus she wroghte:
Among the cursed Jues she him soghte.

She 'frayneth and she preyeth pitously   *implored and begged pitifully*
To every Jew that dwelte in thilke place,
To telle hire if hir child 'went oght forby.   *had passed by at all*
They seide 'nay', but Jhesu, of his grace,
'Yaf in hir thoght, inwith a litel space,   *put into her mind, after a little time*
That in that place after hir sone she cride,
'Where he was casten in a pit biside.   *near by the pit where he had been cast away.*

O grete God, 'that parfournest thy laude   *whose praises are proclaimed*
By mouth of innocentz, lo, 'heere thy might!   *hear of your power!*
This 'gemme of chastite, this ''emeraude,   *pure jewel, emerald*
And eek of 'martirdom the ruby bright,   *bright ruby of martyrdom*
Ther he with 'throte ykorven lay upright,   *with his throat cut*
He 'Alma redemptoris gan to singe   *began to sing 'Mother of our Redeemer'**

So loude that al the place gan to ringe.
* The first words of a church Advent anthem, sung in the days before Christmas.

From *The Nun's Priest's Tale*

Chaucer frequently described courtly relationships, not only presenting the standard behaviour of an aristocratic male and his beloved, but also suggesting some way in which his courtly lovers differed from the conventional image. In *The Nun's Priest's Tale,* set in and around the yard of a poor old woman, the 'courtly couple' are actually a cockerel and his favourite hen, splendidly named Chauntecleer and Pertelote. The aura of chivalric brilliance, given to these fowls, is captured here.

His 'coomb was redder than the fyn coral,	*cockscomb*
And 'batailled as it were a castel wall;	*shaped like the battlements of a castle wall*
His byle was blak, and 'as the jeet it shoon;	*shone like jet*
'Lyk asure were his legges and his "toon;	*blue as the sky, toes*
His 'nayles whitter than the lylye flour,	*claws*
'And lyk the burned gold was his colour.	*and his colour was like burnished gold*
This 'gentil cok hadde in his "governaunce	*noble, control*
'Sevene hennes for to doon al his plesaunce,	*seven hens, provided for his pleasure*
Which were his sustres and his 'paramours,	*lovers*
And 'wonder lyk to him as of colours;	*marvellously similar*
Of which the faireste hewed on hir 'throte	*neck*
Was cleped faire Damoisele Pertelote.	
'Curteys she was, "discreet and debonaire,	*gracious, wise and pleasing*
And compaignable, and 'bar hyrself so faire	*behaved so delightfully*
'Syn thilke day that she was seven nyght oold,	*since the very day*
That trewely she 'hath the herte in hoold	*she had won the heart*
Of Chauntecleer, 'loken in every lith;	*ensnared by every part of her*
He loved hire so that 'wel was hym therwith.	*he was totally happy*
But swich a joye was it to here hem synge,	
Whan that the brighte sonne gan to 'springe,	*rise*
In sweete 'accord, "'My lief is faren in londe!'	*harmony, My love has gone away*
For thilke tyme, as I have understonde,	
'Beestes and briddes koude speke and synge.	*birds and beasts*

The Nun's Priest does not appear in *The General Prologue.* He provides an escort for the Prioress and her sister nuns on their pilgrimage to Canterbury, and remains a shadowy figure. Although we learn very little about him, the story he tells is one of the most accomplished and vivid of *The Canterbury Tales.*

'My lief is faren in londe' – Chauntecleer's song was a popular love song of the age.

My lief is faren in londe	
Allas, why is she so?	
And am so 'sore bonde	*wretchedly confined*
I may not come her to.	
She hath myn herte in holde	
Wherever she ride or go –	
With 'trewe love a thousand-folde.	*the thousand ties of true love*

From *The Franklin's Tale*

Convention decreed that elevated courtly relationships should be essentially romantic attachments; the man pledged undying love and service to his beloved, in return for the smallest of favours. If lover and lady eventually married, the whole affair became much more business-like, the former adoring lover becoming master of the house. The couple in *The Franklin's Tale*, however, attempt to preserve the romantic glow even after their wedding vows; this unconventional contract is put under pressure by events which occur during the tale. This extract, from the beginning of the tale, introduces the lover and lady.

In 'Armorik, that called is ''Britaine,	*Armorica, Brittany*
Ther was a knight that loved and 'dide his paine	*aspired*
To serve a lady 'in his beste wise;	*to the best of his ability*
And many a labour, many a 'greet emprise	*great enterprise*
He for his lady wroghte, er she were wonne.	
For she was 'oon the faireste under sonne,	*one of the fairest*
And eek therto comen of so 'heigh kinrede	*noble family*
That wel 'unnethes dorste this knight, ''for drede,	*scarcely dared, for fear*
Telle hire his wo, his peyne, and his distresse.	
But atte laste she, 'for his worthinesse,	*because he was so very worthy*
And namely for his 'meke obeisaunce,	*meek subservience*
Hath 'swich a pitee caught of his penaunce	*felt such pity for his wretched misery*
That prively she 'fil of his accord	*came to an agreement*
To take him for hir housbonde and hir lord,	
Of 'swich lordshipe as men han over hir wives.	*such lordship as men assert over wives*
And for to lede the 'moore in blisse hir lives,	*in greater joy*
Of his free wil he swoor hire as a knight	
That nevere in al his lyf he, day ne night,	
'Ne sholde upon him take no maistrie	*would he ever assert mastery over her*
Again hire wil, ne 'kithe hire jalousie,	*show jealousy to her*
But hir obeye, and 'folwe hir wil in al,	*do her will always*

As any lovere to his lady shal,
Save that the 'name of soverainetee,   *appearance of mastery*
That wolde he have 'for shame of his degree.   *to preserve his manly status*
She thanked him, and with ful greet humblesse
She seyde, 'Sire, 'sith of youre gentilesse   *since*
Ye profre me to have 'so large a reine,   *such a free rein*
'Ne wolde nevere God bitwixe us tweyne,   *I swear to God never between the two*
                                                        of us

As in 'my gilt, were outher ''werre or stryf.   *for my part, discord or strife*
Sire, I wol be youre humble trewe wyf,
Have heer 'my trouthe, til that myn ''herte breste.'   *my word, heart stops*

From *The Summoner's Tale*

The versatility of Chaucer's rhyming couplets as a means for suggesting the natural rhythms of conversation is apparent in many of *The Canterbury Tales,* not least in the following extract from *The Summoner's Tale.* An urbane friar arrives at the house of a wealthy landowner and his wife, where he is always welcome, and explains to Thomas, master of the house, how hard he has been working since they last met.

I have to day been at youre chirche at 'messe,   *mass*
And 'seyd a sermon after my symple wit,   *gave a sermon in my own simple fashion*
'Nat al after the text of hooly writ;   *not restricted to the Biblical text*
For 'it is hard to yow, as I suppose,   *that would be difficult for you people*
And therfore wol I teche yow al the '*glose.   *interpretation [of the Bible]*
*Glosynge is a glorious thyng, certeyn,
For 'lettre sleeth, so as we clerkes seyn.   *learning is a killer, as we literate men say*
Ther have I taught 'hem to be charitable,   *the flock to be generous*
And 'spende hir good ther it is resonable;   *give their money to some worthwhile*
                                                        cause

And there I saugh 'oure dame – a! where is she?'   *our good lady*
''Yond in the yerd I ''trowe that she be,'   *out in the yard, believe*
Seyde this man, 'and 'she wol come anon.'   *she'll be in directly*
'Ey, maister, welcome be ye, by Seint John!'
Seyde this wyf, ''how fare ye, hertely?'   *lovely to see you, how are you*
The frere ariseth up ful curteisly,
And hire embraceth in his armes 'narwe,   *wiry*
And kiste hire sweete, and 'chirketh as a sparwe   *chirruping like a sparrow*
With his lyppes: 'Dame,' quod he, 'right weel,
As he that is youre servant 'every deel,   *in every way*
Thanked be God, 'that yow yaf soule and lyf!   *that made you, body and soul!*
Yet saugh I nat this day so fair a wyf
In al the chirche, God so save me!'

Glose and *glosynge* (lines 5 and 6) here refer to interpreting the Bible (which was in Latin) for the benefit of uneducated congregations. The words were also used to mean 'deception', an alternative that would not have been lost on Chaucer's audience.

From *The Franklin's Tale*

Chaucer's work is enhanced by an appreciation of natural beauty, the changing seasons and their influence on our spirits. This is combined with an awareness of the fact that our world is part of a much larger system, which also affects us. *The Franklin's Tale* is full of references to astronomy and planetary influences, as well as descriptions of nature, both wild and tamed. This account of the turning of the year contains vivid images of winter, but also marks a crucial turning point in the fortunes of the three main characters – all of whom have debts to pay for promises made earlier.

Upon the morwe, when that it was day,	
To ¹Britaigne tooke they the righte way,	*Britanny*
Aurelius and this magicien ¹biside,	*beside him*
And been descended ther they wolde abide.	
And this was, as ¹thise bookes me remembre,	*the books remind me*
The colde, frosty seson of Decembre.	
¹Phebus wax old, and ¹¹hewed lyk laton,	*the sun grew old, shone like copper*
That in his ¹hoote declinacion	*high, summer position*
Shoon as the ¹burned gold with stremes brighte;	*burnished gold, with bright beams*
But now ¹in Capricorn adoun he lighte,	*under the sign of Capricorn*
Where as he shoon ful ¹pale, I dar wel seyn.	*feebly*
The bittre frostes, with the sleet and reyn,	
Destroyed hath the ¹grene in every yerd.	*greenness in every garden plot*
Janus sit by the fyr, ¹with double berd,	*forked beard*
And drinketh of his bugle horn the wyn;	
¹Biforn him stant brawen of the tusked swyn,	*the Christmas-tide boar's head before him*
And ¹¹'Nowel' crieth every lusty man.	*Nowel [Christ is born]*

Capricorn is the sign of the zodiac believed to govern the period from late December to mid January.

Janus was the mythical deity who presided over the turn of the year. A two-faced god (hence his 'double beard'), he was associated with the feasting that celebrated the twelve days of Christmas. But he also looked forward to the sobriety of January, a time of reckoning.

From *The Knight's Tale*

The Knight's Tale was probably written before the rest of *The Canterbury Tales,* and suggests considerable influence from Boccaccio's poem *Teseida,* written around 1341. War and fighting figure as largely as love: both noble youths have been imprisoned after defeat in battle, and love for the girl they see from their cell destroys their former brotherhood. To decide who should win Emily a huge tournament is fought according to strict rules of chivalry. The fight is dramatic and violent, described in some of the most strongly alliterative verse to be found in *The Canterbury Tales.* The pointlessness of violence is underlined by its result: Palamon is defeated, and Arcite wins the lady; but, through divine intervention, as he triumphs his horse stumbles, and he is mortally injured. Fate has decreed that Emily should be Palamon's.

The heraudes lefte hir ᵗpriking up and doun;	*trotting up and down*
Now ringen ᵗtrompes loude and clarioun.	*trumpets rang out and loud, clarion calls*
Ther is ᵗnamoore to seyn, but west and est	*no more to be said*
In goon the ᵗsperes ful sadly in arrest;	*spears firmly into their sheaths*
In gooth the ᵗsharpe spore into the side.	*sharp spurs jab into the horses' sides*
ᵗTher seen men who kan juste and who kan ride;	*men now see who rides and jousts well*
Ther ᵗshiveren shaftes upon sheeldes thikke:	*spears splinter*
He feeleth ᵗthurgh the herte-spoon the prikke;	*weapon's point through his gut*
Up springen speres twenty foot on highte.	
Out goon the swerdes as the silver brighte;	
The helmes they ᵗtohewen and toshrede;	*batter and tear up*
Out ᵗbrest the blood with stierne stremes rede;	*blood flows in dreadful red streams*
With mighty maces the bones they ᵗtobreste.	*shatter*
ᵗHe thurgh the thikkeste of the throng gan ᵗᵗthreste;	*one man, thrusts*
Ther ᵗstomblen steedes stronge, and ᵗᵗdoun gooth al;	*stumble, all go down*
ᵗHe rolleth under foot as dooth a bal;	*one man*
He ᵗfoyneth on his feet with his ᵗᵗtronchoun,	*lurches to his feet, broken spear shaft*
And ᵗhe him hurtleth with his hors adoun;	*one plunges to earth with his horse*
ᵗHe thurgh the body is hurt and ᵗsithen take,	*one man so is then taken [prisoner]*
ᵗMaugree his heed, and broght unto the ᵗᵗstake;	*despite his objections, resting-stake*
ᵗAs forward was, ᵗᵗright there he moste abide.	*as the rules previously stated,*
	and had to stay there

From *The Miller's Tale*

Following immediately after *The Knight's Tale,* the Miller tells a rollicking *fabliau,* concerning cruel tricks played upon an old carpenter by his lodger, the clerk

Nicholas, and by his unfaithful young wife, Alison. This description of Alison, from *The Miller's Tale,* makes it clear that she stirs up feelings very different from the romantic adoration inspired by noble Emily in the preceding tale.

Fair was this yonge wyf, and therwithal	
¹As any wezele hir body gent and smal.	*a body as supple and slim as a weasel's*
A ¹ceint she werede, ¹¹barred al of silk,	*sash, all striped with silk*
A ¹barmclooth eek as whit as morne milk	*apron*
¹Upon hir lendes, ¹¹ful of many a goore.	*over her hips, finely pleated*
Whit was hir smok, and ¹broiden al bifoore	*embroidered down the front*
And eek bihinde, ¹on hir coler aboute,	*round the collar*
Of col-blak silk, withinne and eek withoute.	
The ¹tapes of hir white voluper	*ribbons of her white cap*
Were of the ¹same suite of hir coler;	*matched her collar*
Hir ¹filet brood of silk, and set ful hye.	*wide, silk headband*
And ¹sikerly she hadde a ¹¹likerous ye;	*truly, wanton eye*
¹Ful smale ypulled were hire browes two,	*most finely plucked*
And tho were ¹bent and ¹¹blake as any sloo.	*arched, black as any sloe*
She was ¹ful moore blisful on to see	*even more of a pleasure for a man to see*
Than is the ¹newe pere-jonette tree,	*young pear tree in blossom*
And softer than the ¹wolle is of a wether.	*wool of a young sheep*
And by hir girdel ¹heeng a purs of lether,	*hung a leather purse*
Tasseled with silk, and ¹perled with latoun.	*shiny brass decorations*
¹In al this world, to seken up and doun,	*if you searched the whole wide world*
There nis no man so wys that koude ¹thenche	*imagine*
So ¹gay a popelote or swich a wenche.	*sprightly a poppet*
Ful brighter was the ¹shining of hir hewe	*radiance of her complexion*
Than ¹in the Tour the noble yforged newe.	*shiny new noble, fresh minted in the Tower*
But of hir song, it was as loude and ¹yerne	*eager*
As any ¹swalwe sittinge on a ¹¹berne.	*swallow, barn*
Therto she koude skippe and make game,	
As any kide or calf folwinge his dame.	
Hir mouth was sweete as ¹bragot or the meeth,	*bragget [ale and honey mixed] or mead*
Or hoord of apples ¹leyd in hey or heeth.	*stored in hay or heather*
¹Winsinge she was, as is a joly colt,	*frisky and skittish*
¹Long as a mast, and upright as a ¹¹bolt.	*upright as a ship's mast,*
	bolt of a crossbow
A brooch she baar upon ¹hir lowe coler,	*the base of her collar*
As brood as is the ¹boos of a bokeler.	*boss of a shield*
Hir shoes were ¹laced on hir legges hye,	*laced high up her legs*
She was a ¹primerole, a ¹¹piggesnie,	*primrose, little cracker*
For any lord to ¹leggen in his bedde,	*take to bed*
Or yet for any good yeman to wedde.	

From *Retractions*

The section known as Chaucer's *Retractions* is usually found at the end of *The Canterbury Tales,* following on from *The Parson's Tale.* The journey to Canterbury is almost over; there are, apparently, no more tales to be told.

HEERE TAKETH THE MAKERE OF THIS BOOK HIS LEVE

Now preye I to hem alle that herkne this litel tretys *[little treatise]*… that if ther be any thyng in it that liketh hem *[pleases them]*, that… they thanken oure Lord Jhesu Crist, of whom procedeth al wit and al goodnesse. And if ther be any thyng that displese hem, I preye hem …they arrette it *[put it down]* to the defaute of myn unkonnynge *[my lack of skill]*, and nat to my wyl, that wolde ful fayn *[would most gladly]* have seyd bettre… For oure book seith, 'Al that is writen is writen for oure doctrine *[instruction]*, and that is myn entente. Wherfore I biseke *[beseech]* yow… for the mercy of God, that ye preye for me that Crist… foryeve me my giltes *[sins]*; and namely of my translacions and enditynges of worldly vanitees *[writings about worldly vanities]*, the whiche I revoke *[set aside]* in my retracciouns: as is the book of Troilus; the book also of Fame;… the book of the Duchesse;… the Parlement of Briddes *[birds]*; the tales of Caunterbury, thilke that sownen into synne *[seem to be sinful]*;… and many another book… and many a song and many a leccherous lay;… Crist for his grete mercy foryeve me… But of the translacion of Boece de Consolacione, and othere bookes of… seintes,… omelies *[homilies]*,… moralitee, and devocioun, that thanke I oure Lord… and his blisful Mooder *[blessed Mother]*, and alle the seintes of hevene, bisekynge hem that they from hennes forth *[now on]*… sende me grace to biwayle my giltes *[repent my sins]*, and to studie to the salvacioun of my soule, and graunte me grace of verray *[true]* penitence, confessioun and satisfaccioun to doon in this present lyf, thurgh the benigne grace of hym that is kyng of kynges… that boghte us with the precious blood of his herte; so that I may be oon of hem at the day of doom *[day of judgement]* that shulle be saved…

HERE IS ENDED THE BOOK OF THE TALES OF CAUNTERBURY, COMPILED BY GEFFREY CHAUCER, OF WHOS SOULE JHESU CRIST HAVE MERCY. AMEN

THE AGE OF CHAUCER

The Gawain poet

From *Sir Gawain and the Green Knight*

Sir Gawain and the Green Knight is another poem of romance and chivalry that reaches its climax with an exciting battle. After challenging King Arthur and his knights to single combat, the Green Knight had been beheaded by one sweep of Gawain's sword. Replacing his head, he departed, demanding Gawain should meet him in a year's time for a return fight. Gawain travelled far to keep his pledge, spending the Christmas season as guest of a hospitable stranger lord and his lady. Whilst the lord hunts in his forests, Gawain indulges in the risky occupation of courting the beautiful wife at home. At New Year Gawain is guided to the Green Chapel, where his fate, in the shape of the Green Knight, awaits him.

Then the 'gome in the grene graythed hym swythe,	*man in green braced himself*
'Gederes up hys grymme tole, Gawayn to ''smyte;	*swept up his grim blade, hit*
With alle the 'bur in his body he ''ber hit on lofte,	*strength, swung it up*
'Munt as maghtyly as marre hym he wolde.	*aiming as fiercely as if to maim him*
Hade hit dryven adoun 'as drey as he atled	*as hard as he seemed to*
Ther 'hade ben ded of his ''dynt that doghty was ever.	*would have died, split by the force*
But Gawayn on that 'giserne glyfte hym bysyde	*glimpsed the axe stroke*
As hit 'com glydande adoun on ''glode hym to schende	*swung down, meaning to destroy him*
And 'schranke a lytel with the schulderes for the scharp ''yrne.	*flinched his shoulders, iron*
That other 'schalk ''wyth a schunt the schene wythhaldes,	*foe, jerked his blade away*
And thenne 'repreved he the prynce with mony prowde wordes:	*reproved the prince*
'Thou art not Gawayn,' quoth the gome, 'that is 'so goud halden,	*of such great renown*
That never 'arwed for no here by hylle ne be vale,	*feared no army by hill or vale*
And now thou 'fles for ferde er thou ''fele harmes.	*flinch for fear, feel a blow*
Such cowardise of that knyght cowthe 'I never here.	*I never knew*
Nawther 'fyked I ne flaghe, freke, ''quen thou myntest,	*flinched nor fled, when you hurt me*
Ne 'kest no kavelacion in kynges hous Arthor.	*raised an objection in Arthur's court*
My hede 'flaw to my fote and yet ''flagh I never;	*fell at my feet, winced*
And thou, 'er any harme hent, ''arwes in hert.	*before you're even touched, wince away*

Wherfore the 'better burne me burde be called	*must be considered the better warrior*
Therfore.'	
Quoth Gawayn, 'I 'schunt ones,	*flinched once*
And so wyl I no more;	
But 'thagh my hede falle on the stones,	*if my head falls on the stones*
I con not hit restore.'	

Notice the strong alliterative element in this passage – the poem depends on this rather than any rhyme scheme – and also on the caesura, or break, in the middle of each line. Further rhythmic variation is gained from the shorter lines, at the end of the passage, which act as a division and also a summary of each section.

Anonymous

From a *York Mystery Play*

This play was traditionally (and appropriately) performed by the fishers and mariners. The play was written in 14-line stanzas, sufficiently flexible to convey lively dialogue. Here, in the story of Noah's ark, only slightly modernised for today's audiences, Mrs. Noah refuses to get on his ridiculous ark without her pots and pans:

NOAH	Dame, forty days are near-hand past	
	And gone since it began to rain,	
	'On life shall no man longer last	*no man will be left alive*
	But we alone, 'is not to lain.	*this is not to be disguised*
WIFE	Now, Noah, in faith thou 'fons full fast,	*behave like an idiot*
	'This fare will I no longer frayne;	*I refuse to hear more [about this business]*
	Thou art 'near wood, I am aghast,	*you're practically mad*
	Farewell, I will go home again.	
NOAH	Oh, woman, art thou 'wood?	*mad*
	Of my works thou 'nought wot;	*know nothing*
	'All that has bone or blood	*every living thing*
	Shall be overflowed with the flood.	
WIFE	In faith, thou 'were as good	*you might as well*
	To let me 'go my gate.	*go my own way*
	'We! Out! Harrow!	*Help! Get away! Be off!*
NOAH	What now, what cheer?	
WIFE	'I will no nar for no-kins need.	*I shan't stay here for anything*
NOAH	Help, my sons, to hold her here,	

	For 'to her harms she takes no heed.	*to the danger she's in*
SON	Be merry mother, and 'mend your cheer;	*change your attitude*
	This world be drowned, 'without dread.	*without doubt*
WIFE	Alas, that I 'this lore should lere.	*this fact should learn*
NOAH	Thou 'spills us all, ill might thou speed.	*be the death of us all, if you don't hurry up.*
SON 2	Dear mother, 'won with us,	*stay*
	'There shall nothing you grieve.	*you won't be sorry if you do*
WIFE	Nay, 'needlings home me bus,	*I've got to go home*
	For I have 'tools to truss.	*pack up my kitchen things*
NOAH	Woman, why does thou thus?	
	To make us more mischief?	
WIFE	Noah, thou might have' let me wit.	*let me know*
	Early and late thou went thereout,	
	And ay at home thou let me sit	
	'To look that nowhere were well about.	*staring at nothing*
NOAH	Dame, thou hold me excused of it,	
	It was God's will without doubt.	
WIFE	What, 'weens thou so for to go quit?	*do you think you're going to get out of it like that?*
	Nay, by my troth, 'thou gets a clout.	*I'll box your ears*

From an early fifteenth century song

The misfortune of marrying a dominant, older wife is the subject matter of this song. Clearly the comic image of hen-pecked husbands is not new.

'Ying men, O warne you everychon,	*young*
'Elde wyvys tak ye non,	*marry no old wives*
'For I myself have on at hom:	*I have one of those at home*
'I dar not seyn quan she seyth 'Pes!'	*I dare not speak a word when she says 'shut up!'*
Quan I cum fro the plow at non,	
In a 'reven dysh myn mete is don;	*broken bowl*
I dar not askyn our dame 'a spon	*for a spoon*
I dar not seyn quan she seyth 'Pes!'	
If I aske our dame 'bred,	*for bread*
She takyt a staf and brekit myn hed	
And doth me 'rennyn undir the bed:	*running to hide under the bed*
I dar not seyn quan she seyth 'Pes!'	

Song of the period

Another fine cockerel, similar to Chauntecleer, appears in an anonymous song of the period, in which the sexual implications are more obvious:

I have a gentil cok, 'crowyt me the day;	*crows at daybreak*
He 'doth me rysyn erly my matyns for to say.	*makes me rise early to say my morning prayers*
I have a gentyl cok, 'comyn he is of gret;	*very highly bred*
His comb is of reed corel, his tayl is of get.	
I have a gentyl cok, 'comyn he is of kynde;	*he is well born*
His comb is of red corel, his tayl is 'of inde.	*indigo*
His leggis ben of 'asour, so "gentil and so smale,	*sky-blue, elegant and slender*
'His sporis arn of sylvir qwyt into the worte-wale.	*his spurs silver-white at the base*
His 'eynyn arn of crystal lokyn al in aumbyr,	*eyes gleam in crystal and amber*
And every nyghte he 'perchit hym	*perches*
in myn ladyis chaumbyr.	

4 | Critical approaches

- How was Chaucer viewed in the fifteenth century?

- How have attitudes to medieval literature (and to Chaucer, in particular) changed in the intervening centuries?

Chaucer's reputation in the fifteenth and sixteenth centuries

Chaucer's immediate successors evidently regarded him as the most important fourteenth century poet. Gower and Lydgate were also admired, but it was Chaucer who was the most influential and most widely imitated by other writers. He was seen, primarily, as the writer who established English as a literary language. The invention of the printing press had enormous influence in promoting literary works; William Caxton published two editions of *The Canterbury Tales,* in 1478 and 1485. His *proem* [prologue] to the second edition establishes his reasons for holding Chaucer in such high regard:

> …in especial tofore alle other we ought to gyve a synguler laude *[particular praise]* unto that noble and grete philosopher Gefferey Chaucer, the whiche for his ornate wrytyng in our tongue may wel have the name of a laureate poete. For tofore *[for the reason]* that he by hys labour enbelysshyd, ornated, and made faire *[embellished, dignified and made beautiful]* our Englisshe, in thys royame was had rude speche and incongrue *[in this realm which previously had a rough and outlandish sort of speech]*, as yet it appiereth by olde bookes whyche at thys day ought not to have place ne be compared emong ne to hys beauteuous volumes and aournate writynges *[elegant works]*; of whom he made many bokes and treatyces of many a noble historye, as wel in metre as in ryme and prose, and them so craftyly made that he comprehended hys maters in short, quyck, and hye sentences *[briefly, succinctly and with deep meaning]*, eschewyng prolyxyte *[avoiding verbosity]*, castyng away the chaf *[chaff]* of superfluyte, and shewyng the pyked grayn *[well chosen essence]* of sentence utteryd by crafty and sugred eloquence; of whom emonge all other of hys bokes I purpose t'emprynte, by the grace of God, the *Book of the Tales of Cauntyrburye,* in whiche I fynde many a noble hystorye of every astate and degre *[type and degree of people]*, fyrst rehercyng the condicions and th'arraye of eche of them as properly as possyble is to be sayd, and after theyr

tales, whyche ben of noblesse, wysedom, gentylesse, myrthe, and also of veray holynesse and vertue, wherin he fynysshyth thys sayd booke;

▶ What does Caxton find particularly praiseworthy about both the style and content of Chaucer's works? Find your own examples to justify his comments.

Gower and Chaucer had been friends who influenced each other in choice of subject matter and style; Hoccleve and Lydgate confirm Chaucer's status as the greatest poet of his age by adopting his verse form and subject matter, and through outright praise and a determination to link their works to his own. Here Thomas Hoccleve acknowledges Chaucer as his master in a work of 1411:

My dere mayster – God hys soule quyte! –
And fadir, Chaucer, fayn wolde han me taght,
But I was dul, and lerned lyte or naght.

Alas! my worthy mayster honorable,
Thys landes verray tresour and rychesse,
Deth, by thy deth, hath harme irreparable
Unto us don; hir vengeable duresse
Despoyled hath this land of the swetnesse
Of rethorik, for unto Tullius
Was never man so lyk amonges us.

Also, who was heir in philosophye
To Aristotle in our tonge but thou?
The steppes of Virgile in poesie
Thow filwedist eek.

My dear master – God save his soul! –
and father, Chaucer, wished to teach me,
but I was stupid, and learned little or nothing.

Sadly, my worthy and honourable master,
the true treasure and jewel of this country,
Death, by your death, has done irreparable harm
to us; her ruthless vengeance
has stripped this country of the sweetness
of fine writing [rhetoric], for never was any other
man amongst us so like Tullius.

Moreover, who but you could claim to be heir
to Aristotle in our language?
And in poetic skill you also followed
in the steps of Virgil.

▶ Why might Hoccleve claim to be so particularly grateful to Chaucer?

In the Prologue to his poem of 1422 *The Siege of Thebes,* Lydgate displays his debt
to Chaucer, and the continued popularity of *The Canterbury Tales,* by assuming
the role of one of the storytellers on the journey to Canterbury:

> Whan Aurora was in the morowe red,
> And Jubiter in the Crabbes hed
> Hath taken his paleys and his mansioun –
> The lusty tyme and joly fressh sesoun
> Whan that Flora, the noble myghty quene,
> The soyl hath clad in newe tendre grene
> With her floures craftyly ymeynt,
> Braunch and bough with red and whit depeynt,
> Fletinge the bawme on hillis and on valys –
> The tyme in soth whan Canterbury talys
> Complet and told at many sondry stage
> Of estatis in the pilgrimage,
> Everich man lik to his degre –
> Some of desport, some of moralite,
> Som of knyghthode, love and gentillesse,
> and some also of parfit holynesse,
> And some also in soth of ribaudye
> To make laughter in the companye…

> *When the sun shone red in the morning,*
> *and Jupiter in the astrological mansion of Cancer*
> *had taken up his position –*
> *the lively time and pleasant fresh season*
> *when Flora, noble powerful goddess of spring*
> *had covered the soil in new delicate green*
> *mingled subtly with her flowers,*
> *painted branches and boughs with red and white,*
> *wafted spring scents over hills and vales –*
> *that time, in truth, when Canterbury tales*
> *were composed and told at various stages*
> *by the various types on the pilgrimage,*

every man according to his status –
some told of sport, some morality,
some of knighthood, love and gentillesse,
some of absolute holiness,
and some, in truth, of ribald things
to make the group laugh…

▶ Look back to the opening lines of Chaucer's *General Prologue* on page 8. How closely does Lydgate imitate it here? Which seems to you the better piece of writing, and why?

Lydgate continues his prologue with lines which echo many of the sentiments of both Caxton and Hoccleve:

…Floure of poetes thorghout al Breteyne,
Which sothly hadde most of excellence
In rethorike and in eloquence
(Rede his making, who list the trouthe fynde),
Which never shal appallen in my mynde
But alwey fressh ben in my memoyre.
To who be yove pris, honure and gloyre
Of wel-seyinge first in oure langage,

Flower of poets through all Britain,
who truly was the most excellent
in rhetoric and eloquence
(read his writings, whoever wishes to discover the truth)
his works shall never fade from my mind
but always be fresh in my memory.
To you be given praise, honour and glory
as the first great speaker in our language.

By the mid to late fifteenth century English had rapidly become more established and crafted as a language; inevitably, Chaucer and his contemporaries began to sound old-fashioned and clumsy. His subject matter – courtly romances, tales of chivalry and *gentillesse* – remained popular for some time, as seen in the *Morte d'Arthur* of Sir Thomas Malory (c.1410–1471) and in the *Testament of Cressid,* written by the Scottish poet, Robert Henryson, probably in the 1490s. He and his fellow Scot, William Dunbar, were sometimes known as the 'Scottish Chaucerians' for their admiration for Chaucer, in particular his *Troilus and Criseyde*. Dunbar spoke of 'noble Chaucer, of makaris flour' [the flower of all creative writers]. John

Skelton, writing c.1505, in a poetic lament over deceased Philip Sparrow (a pet bird) clearly views Chaucer as the greatest of the medieval poets, although his assessment of Chaucer's language seems a mite condescending:

> In Chauser I am sped,
> His tales have I red;
> His mater is delectable,
> Solacious and commendable;
> His Englysh well alowed,
> So as it is enprowed,
> For as it is enployd
> There is no Englysh voyd
> At those dayes moch commended.

> *I am very familiar with Chaucer,*
> *I have read his stories;*
> *his subject matter is delightful,*
> *comforting and commendable,*
> *his use of English effective,*
> *so that it is put to good use,*
> *for the manner in which he writes*
> *means there are no superfluous words*
> *a thing much valued in those days.*

Certainly Chaucer's influence on literature of the sixteenth century waned rapidly, as his vocabulary appeared increasingly quaint and archaic. An edition of his works produced in 1598 contained, for the first time, a glossary of 'old and obscure words'. As the quality and inventiveness of English literature flourished in all directions, few were impressed by older medieval poetry.

Writing in the reign of the Protestant Elizabeth I, the acclaimed poet Edmund Spenser (1552–1599) saw in Chaucer (and Langland) writers sympathetic towards Wyclif and his ideas, and also critical of aspects of the Catholic church of their age. They offered, therefore, vindication for supporters of Elizabeth's Protestant church:

> Dan Chaucer, well of English undefyled
> On Fame's eternal beadroll worthie to be fyled.

Spenser adopted the alliterative style and old-fashioned vocabulary associated with Chaucer in his *Shepherd's Calendar* and *Faerie Queene,* an allegory in which the Red Cross Knight wages war against the children of Error, a metaphor for the persistent influence of the Catholic church. He admired Chaucer not for his poetic skills, nor especially for his tales of courtly love, but as a critic of the Catholic church.

'Refining' Chaucer

The Restoration period, after 1660, was a time of elegance and sophistication. Classical architecture, art and literature provided inspiration for cultured life, and Chaucer's language was disregarded as rough and crude, though he was applauded for his skill in taking classical sources, such as Ovid, as his inspiration. He had admirers, particularly Dryden, who rewrote some *Canterbury Tales* in 1700. Dryden's Preface to his *Fables Ancient and Modern* shows penetrating critical appreciation of many aspects of Chaucer's work. He apologises to fellow writers and critics, who might consider him mad for preferring Chaucer to Ovid, stating he found Ovid 'full of flashy jingles and conceits', whereas Chaucer 'writ with more Simplicity and follow'd Nature more closely'. In his dedication to the *Fables* it is clear that what Dryden believes makes Chaucer great is his resemblance to the classical poets:

> The Bard who first adorn'd our native tongue
> Tun'd to his British lyre this ancient song;
> Which Homer might without a blush reherse,
> And leaves a doubtful palm in Virgil's verse;
> He match'd their beauties, where they most excell;
> Of Love sung better, and of Arms as well.

But Dryden sees him as a 'rough Diamond, and must first be polish'd e'er he shines', taking upon himself the task of polishing. Having praised Chaucer's ability to describe 'various Manners and Humours' of medieval society in his *General Prologue,* Dryden commends the skill with which the tales are allocated to appropriate tellers, and informs his readers that he has chosen to re-tell only those tales that 'savour nothing of Immodesty' – no *Miller's* or *Reeve's Tale,* for example.

▶ The story of Palamon and Arcite, or *The Knight's Tale,* is one Dryden considers acceptable. Compare the passage below with the corresponding passage from Chaucer on page 83 in Part 3. Have Dryden's alterations improved on the original, in choice of language and tone? Does he seem to have lost some aspect of Chaucer's original?

> If Love be passion, and that passion nurst
> With strong desires, I lov'd the Lady first.
> Canst thou pretend desire, whom zeal inflam'd
> To worship, and a pow'r celestial nam'd?
> Thine was devotion to the blest above,
> I saw the woman, and desir'd her love;
> First own'd my passion, and to thee commend

Th'important secret, as my chosen friend.
Suppose (which yet I grant not) thy desire
A moment elder than my rival fire:
Can chance of seeing first thy title prove?
And know'st thou not, no law is made for love?
Law is to things which to free choice relate:
Love is not in our choice, but in our fate:
Laws are but positive: Love's pow'r we see
Is nature's sanction, and her first decree.
Each day we break the bond of human laws
For Love, and vindicate the common cause.
Laws for defence of civil rights are plac'd,
Love throws the fences down, and makes a general waste:
Maids, widows, wives, without distinction fall;
The sweeping deluge, Love, comes on and covers all.
If then the laws of friendship I transgress,
I keep the greater, while I break the less;
And both are mad alike, since neither can possess.
Both hopeless to be ransom'd, never more
To see the sun, but as he passes o'er.
Like Esop's hounds contending for the bone,
Each pleaded right, and wou'd be lord alone;
The fruitless fight continu'd all the day,
A cur came by and snatch'd the prize away.

The Pre-Raphaelites: medieval revival

The urge to 'improve' Chaucer by translating his works, chiefly *Troilus and Criseyde* and *The Canterbury Tales,* persisted; and appreciation of his poetic skills, as opposed to his story-telling, seemed almost non-existent until nineteenth century writers began to read medieval texts, particularly Chaucer, in the original. Some of Keats' most famous poems – *Lamia, Isabella, The Eve of St. Agnes, La Belle Dame sans Merci* – published in 1820, had themes relating to knighthood and chivalry. Keats had admired the works of Chatterton, the boy poet who posed as a fifteenth century monk in his writings, and had adopted a Chaucerian vocabulary. Tennyson used the medieval tales of Arthur and his Round Table knights as inspiration for his *Morte d'Arthur* of 1842 and the *Idylls of the King,* first published in 1859.

With the founding of the Pre-Raphaelite brotherhood in 1848, the Victorian love affair with the medieval world reached its height. Led by a small group of poets and artists, including Dante Gabriel Rossetti and John Millais, the Pre-Raphaelites (called so because they favoured earlier painters like Giotto, Fra Angelico and

Ghirlandaio) were joined by such influential talented men as Ford Madox Brown, Edward Burne-Jones and William Morris. The Pre-Raphaelites advocated a return to a 'medieval purity of vision'; in an age of industrial development they looked back nostalgically to the fourteenth century, as a time when men were closer to nature, and life was simpler, purer and brighter. Their admiration for all things medieval manifested itself not just in paintings and literature but also in tapestries, carvings, stained glass window designs, and furniture and architecture. Two paintings by Ford Madox Brown – *Wyclif reading from his translation of the New Testament to John of Gaunt,* and *Chaucer reading the Legend of Custance at the court of Edward III* – indicate their deep interest in medieval writers. Chaucer's early poems were particularly admired – those concerned with courtly love, noble knights and dream fantasies. William Morris took Chaucer as his inspiration, seeing him as a gentleman poet, and a visionary, removed from the turmoil of everyday life, the first to bring classical and European influences to the English language. In his epic, *The Earthly Paradise* (1868–1870), a group of wandering mariners search for a Western Land far from the stress and tension of contemporary life, and as they travel they tell one another stories, in the Chaucerian manner:

> Forget six counties overhung with smoke,
> Forget the snorting steam and piston stroke,
> Forget the spreading of the hideous town;
> Think rather of the pack-horse on the down,
> And dream of London, small and white, and clean,
> The clear Thames bordered by its gardens green…

▶ In what way does Morris' attitude towards the London he sees in the nineteenth century colour his view of Chaucer's London? Would Chaucer have agreed, do you think, with his view of London as 'small and white and clean'? How accurate is the view of Chaucer as a dreamy, courtly poet, uninvolved in the tensions of his world?

The Kelmscott Press, named after the Oxfordshire manor house shared by Morris and Rossetti, and Morris' Hammersmith home of the same name, published exquisitely presented editions of early English texts during the 1890s. The most famous is *The Kelmscott Chaucer,* illustrated by Burne-Jones. Both the designer, Morris, and the artist, Burne-Jones, chose to emphasise Chaucer the nature poet; in their hands *The Canterbury Tales* became a harmonious stroll through the leafy Kentish countryside. The robust humour of the *fabliau* has no place here.

Other writers also found inspiration from Chaucer's works. The American poet, Henry Wadsworth Longfellow, subscribed to Morris' view of Chaucer as a 'nature' poet. In 1863 he published *Tales of a Wayside Inn,* which imitated *The Canterbury*

Tales in that they were a collection of stories, but, unlike Chaucer's work, made no attempt to heighten interest or complexity by characterisation of the narrators. Longfellow looked back on the fourteenth century with a yearning for escape from the modern world similar to that of the Pre-Raphaelites; for him the *Tales* evoked the calls:

> of lark and linnet, and from every page
> Rose odours of ploughed field or flowery mead.

The Irish poet W. B. Yeats (1865–1939) was stimulated by Chaucer's early love stories and dream fantasies when writing his early poetry about Irish myths and legends. Yeats praised Chaucer not for the 'harmonious' nature of his *Canterbury Tales* but for the variety of tales and tellers, recognising that Chaucer deliberately juxtaposed comedy and tragedy, low life and chivalry, since both extremes were part of the world he knew. The importance of the oral element in Irish literature no doubt enabled Yeats to appreciate the vitality and flow of 'writers like Chaucer, who wrote essentially for the ear'; he particularly admired the aptness of Chaucer's description:

> … Chaucer in that same unspeakable tale *[The Miller's Tale]* calls a certain young wife 'white and small as a weasel'. Does it not bring the physical type clearly to the mind's eye? I think one wants that sort of vivid irresistible phrase in all verse to be spoken aloud – it rests the imagination as upon the green ground.

▶ Yeats has captured the gist of the description, if not the exact words (see Part 3, page 91). What do the two words 'weasel' and 'white' suggest particularly to you about the young wife? Are there any words or phrases from a piece of Chaucer that you know well that you have found especially vivid and irresistible?

In spite of the reverence and praise of perceptive critics such as these, as well as attempts to engender enthusiasm for his works by the Chaucer Society, founded in 1868, Chaucer's standing in the literary world remained relatively low. The writer and critic Leigh Hunt called him 'a rude sort of poet, who wrote a vast while ago, and is no longer intelligible.'

The 'Englishness' of Chaucer

In the first part of the twentieth century, there were attempts to make Chaucer into both an author for children and a patriotic symbol. Books such as *Tales of the Canterbury Pilgrims* (1904), retold by Harvey Darton and profusely illustrated, contained heavily abridged versions of the tales, set in some vague and distant past. By the 1930s versions of the *fabliaux* were included, heavily censored. The impression given was that Chaucer was a jolly, lively fun-loving sort of scamp, a fit model for English schoolboy readers four hundred years on. Darton describes Chaucer as 'a little elvish-looking fellow – as bright and quick as a boy could be, plucky and slippy at football, hockey, and other games'.

▶ Take any Chaucerian tale you know well and decide how it would need to be altered to adapt it into a story for younger readers. What would be lost in the alterations? What might be gained?

In the period during and between the two World Wars, English literature often became a vehicle for promoting patriotism. Shakespeare was a perfect example; the film of *Henry V* made in 1943 with Laurence Olivier as Henry, was a nationalistic battle cry. It was less easy to brand Chaucer as a patriot in the same way, since devotion to his country is rarely, if ever, expressed in his work. Nevertheless, in 1944 the film *A Canterbury Tale* by Michael Powell and Emeric Pressburger opened with a view of the travelling pilgrims and a recital of the first lines of *The General Prologue,* to be replaced by the sights and sounds of the Second World War. Chaucer's poem represented here a nostalgic view of a country threatened by the horrors of war. A feeling developed that the personality of the poet, discernible in his writings, made him somehow the quintessential Englishman, who wrote about a motley group of essentially English characters wandering along country lanes in the English spring time. Chaucer's image became that of a simple, straightforward, quietly humorous country gentleman, not too intellectual. One of his greatest admirers in the 1930s was G.K. Chesterton:

> There was never a man who was more of a Maker than Chaucer. He made a national language; he came very near to making a nation. Chaucer was the Father of his Country, rather in the style of George Washington. And apart from that, he made something that has altered all Europe more than the Newspaper: the Novel.

▶ In what way did Chaucer 'make the Novel'?

In *Dan Chaucer,* H.D. Sedgwick, the American critic, enthusiastically endorsed this notion of Chaucer's Englishness, and the writer as a supreme example of the national temperament, whose scholarship is worn lightly: 'primarily a human being… and but secondly a poet'. Virginia Woolf, in her critical essays of 1925, *The Common Reader,* saw Chaucer as a writer capable of capturing the images of the simple life 'out of doors' – '…cocks and hens, millers, old peasant women, flowers – …common things…'

▶ Look again at one of the passages in Part 3 that deal with 'common life' – that from *The Nun's Priest's Tale* or the description of Alison from *The Miller's Tale*. Do you feel that the passage supports the comments of those critics who see Chaucer as the embodiment of Englishness? How often, for example, does Chaucer write about rural matters?

Woolf also stressed Chaucer's gift for story-telling: 'For the storyteller, besides his indescribable zest for facts, must tell his story craftily, without undue stress or excitement, or we shall swallow it whole and jumble the parts together; he must let us stop, give us time to think and look about us, yet always be persuading us to move on.'

Recent developments in Chaucer criticism

The twentieth century saw increasing scholarly interest in Chaucer, in America and Britain. Closer focus on the language of the fourteenth century promoted deeper respect for and understanding of the text. He is no longer seen as the 'rough diamond' of Dryden's assessment. The care with which Chaucer uses language and telling detail has become part of the way in which his writing is evaluated. The word *wenche,* for example, never appears in his descriptions of well-born females. Some words, such as *gentil,* may be used satirically, or with true seriousness. The word *hende,* meaning both 'nice' and 'handy' or 'close to hand' is used, apparently blandly, in the first description of the young lodger-student, Nicholas, in *The Miller's Tale,* but takes on greater resonance as the handsome young man smooth-talks his way into his landlady's bed.

Research has given greater insight into the historical and cultural background, and thus greater understanding of Chaucer's works. We have more grasp of issues that preoccupied fourteenth century people – such things as the place of women in society, power structures in individual relationships, the extent to which the church could and should control lives, the opportunities available to alter one's social status. Paul Strohm's *Social Chaucer* (1989) looks at the way the *Tales* reflect the social diversity of the time. Research into the activities of crusading knights has led one modern critic, Terry Jones, in *Chaucer's Knight: The Portrait* of *a Medieval Mercenary* (1980), to see the Knight's depiction in *The General Prologue* as little more than an ironic piece of whitewash, a view roundly disputed by others. Academic interest in medieval literature flourishes.

G.L. Kittredge, an American scholar, was one who emphasised the importance of the variety of personalities involved in the Canterbury tale-telling:

> Structurally regarded, the *Canterbury Tales* is a kind of Human Comedy. From this point of view, the Pilgrims are the *dramatis*

personae, and their stories are only speeches that are somewhat longer than common, entertaining in and for themselves (to be sure), but primarily significant, in each case, because they illustrate the speaker's character and opinions, or show the relations of the travellers to one another in the progressive action of the Pilgrimage.

It was Kittredge who first suggested the view of *The Canterbury Tales* as a promenade of characters, with traits recognisable in their modern successors. Critics increasingly noted Chaucer's ability to bring characters to life by describing their appearance and behaviour.

Greater familiarity with texts of the fourteenth century and earlier led many to acknowledge the debt Chaucer owed to earlier writers, recognising that 'borrowings' from classical literature and European poetry proved him to be a scholar and man of letters, rather than the unsophisticated 'nature' poet of earlier critics.

Most importantly, perhaps, many see Chaucer as firmly established as a writer who reveals through his works the social and political attitudes of his time. The structure of medieval society was commonly parodied in contemporary literature through a genre known as 'estates satire': idealised images of the main social classes were compared with less than perfect examples to be found in real life. In her book published in 1973, *Chaucer and Medieval Estates Satire,* Jill Mann points out that Chaucer's *General Prologue* is as much an example of such satirical fault-finding as it is a straightforward introduction to the tales which follow. There is, however, far more subtlety in Chaucer's descriptions than may be found, for example, in the downright attack on social groups by such writers as Langland. Helen Cooper, in *The Canterbury Tales* in the *Oxford Guides to Chaucer,* indicates the refinement *The General Prologue* brings to the genre:

> Estates satires tended to take the form of invective; Chaucer is the master of irony by way of the superlative. All the pilgrims are the best of their kind; sometimes it is true, but there is no critical unanimity as to just when. The irony furthermore is sometimes much more subtle than an attack on a failure to live up to an ideal. That the Friar is the 'beste beggere in his hous' clearly shows that charity and poverty have gone amiss, but since friars are beggars, there is a certain logic in equating the best beggar with the best friar. The language of the text demands approval; knowledge of the fraternal ideal demands condemnation. The pilgrims are often in part defined by what Chaucer does not say about them, when he writes all around a convention of praise or blame, but leaves an appropriately shaped hole in the middle.

▶ Which other pilgrims from *The General Prologue* can also be said to be defined by 'what Chaucer does not say about them'?

Recent evaluation has noted not only the way Chaucer's writings represent the thoughts and attitudes of the medieval world, about which we now know much more, but also reach out to speak with relevance to later generations. Here, for example, is part of the prologue to *The Franklin's Tale*. The Franklin praises the Squire's tale, telling the assembled company of his ambitions for and concerns about his own son, who is not half as gentlemanly. Unquestionably, this passage had total relevance for Chaucer's original audience, all of whom recognised that a social-climbing, self-made Franklin would want his family to appear *gentil,* but would also disapprove of wasting money. It could also be applicable today:

> ...of thy speche I have greet deyntee.
> I have a sone, and by the Trinitee,
> I hadde levere than twenty pound worth lond,
> Though it right now were fallen in myn hond,
> He were a man of swich discrecioun
> As that ye been. Fy on possessioun,
> But if a man be vertuous withal!
> I have my sone snybbed, and yet shal,
> For he to vertu listeth nat entende;
> But for to pleye at dees, and to despende
> And lese al that he hath, is his usage.
> And he hath levere talken with a page
> Than to comune with any gentil wight
> Where he mighte lerne gentillesse aright.

> *I've really enjoyed your story.*
> *I have a son, and, by the holy Trinity,*
> *rather than being given land worth twenty pounds,*
> *even if it fell into my hand right now,*
> *I wish he was a man of such discerning taste*
> *as you are. Riches are useless,*
> *unless the man who has them is also noble!*
> *I have lectured my son, and will do so again,*
> *because he refuses to take note of wise words;*
> *gambling with dice, wasting his money*
> *and losing all his allowance, is his practice.*
> *And he'd rather talk to a common page*
> *than converse with a cultured person*
> *from whom he might learn true gentillesse.*

Increasingly, *The Canterbury Tales,* or at least sections of them, have received great prominence as suitable material for Advanced Level studies for students of English Literature. Detailed critical study of individual tales has been combined with interest in the manner in which the tales are intermingled. Derek Pearsall indicates the versatility and richness of the mixture here:

> The plan... enabled him to make of the *Canterbury Tales* a vast laboratory of narrative experiment, in which any form or genre or type of tale could be tried out – romances, comic tales, *fabliaux,* religious tales, saints' lives,... a beast-fable... a fairy-tale.... The freedom to experiment with narrative that Chaucer sought and found in this way was not of course an end in itself. What it gave Chaucer was a means to explore in many ways and at many levels of seriousness the issues that preoccupied the society of which he was part.

Some critics point out that the fourteenth century was a period of turmoil and social and political struggle, similar in many ways to the world today. In Paul Strohm's *Social Chaucer* (1989), the writer sees *The Canterbury Tales* as reflecting a wide range of voices from all ranks of society, demanding to make themselves heard, co-existing, but also fighting for their place in society. Debate about social issues ranges across several tales, and the arguments employed invite the reader to take into account the characters involved. For example, some tales make up the group that debate the whole question of marriage. Many other tales also touch upon the balance of power in sexual relationships, and the perceptions of women's roles in society. Feminist criticism of recent years has had much to say about the traditional role of women in medieval society and literature, and the role Chaucer has given to his female characters in his writings. The Wife of Bath, in particular, is seen both as an icon of feminism – fighting for her own voice in a patriarchal world – and also to other critics as a symbol of everything anti-feminists attacked in women. An anthology of feminist criticism *The Authority of Experience* (1977), borrows its title from her first words. In her world spiritual authority and legal power lay in the hands of the male-dominated church and state, and her unstoppable voice throws down a challenge, offering an alternative way of life – but one that has to be fought for:

> Experience, though noon auctoritee
> Were in this world, is right ynogh for me
> To speke of wo that is in mariage;

Her voice is that of a rebel, not just against the domination of men, but, as some critics have noted, against the established church itself: the language she uses contains many echoes of Lollardry, and the *auctoritee* she dismisses is the Biblical and clerical authority delivered every Sunday from the pulpits of the male-dominated Catholic church. Where Chaucer's sympathy lies in this debate remains open to question.

▶ Which other Chaucerian women seem to you to challenge the idea of a male-dominated world?

More recent critics view the Wife as a portrayal of conventional medieval anti-feminism; the latest Chaucer criticism has moved into discussion of broader gender issues, including the question of the Pardoner's homosexuality (see Caroline Dinshaw, *Getting Medieval*, Duke University Press, 1999).

Acknowledgement of Chaucer's interest in spiritual and philosophical issues has taken modern assessment a long way from the jolly Englishman, with no intellectual pretensions, as seen by Sedgwick and Woolf. Although Chaucer gives no explicit moral viewpoint, *The Canterbury Tales* continually invite us to make moral judgements. The first long sentence of *The General Prologue* (see page 8) presents an intermingling of worldly desires and impulses with human yearnings towards some sort of spiritual endeavour. This mixture provides a theme throughout the work, as different tales and tellers reveal all manner of combinations of physical and spiritual decisions through their words and actions. Moral choices frequently form the basis of tales; the importance of *trouthe* – keeping one's word, behaving with honour and virtue – is a recurrent theme. In an earlier ballad, commonly entitled *Trouthe*, Chaucer discusses the human predicament:

> That thee is sent, receyve in buxumnesse;
> The wrastling for this world axeth a fal.
> Her is non hoom, her nis but wildernesse:
> Forth, pilgrim, forth! Forth, beste, out of thy stal!
> Know thy contree, look up, thank God of al;
> Holde the heye wey and lat thy gost thee lede,
> And trouthe thee shal delivere, it is no drede.

> *Take whatever life sends you in obedience;*
> *Struggling for the riches of this world leads to misfortune.*
> *This is not your home, but only a wilderness:*
> *go forward pilgrim! Leave behind earthly desires!*
> *Recognise your ultimate goal, look up, thank God of all*
> *keep to the high road, and be led by your spirit [or soul]*
> *and fear not, for true virtue will save you.*

▶ How aware have you been, in your reading of Chaucer, of his concern with spiritual and moral issues?

Although *The Canterbury Tales* offer a kaleidoscope of stories, that include the bawdy and irreligious as readily as the virtuous, the placing of *The Parson's Tale* is seen as particularly significant, in interpreting the whole work as a vision of humanity journeying towards the inevitable destination. *The Parson's Prologue* emphasises that his is the final voice to be heard, apart from that of the author himself:

> By that the Maunciple hadde his tale al ended,
> The sonne fro the south lyne was descended
> So lowe that he nas nat, to my sighte,
> Degres nyne and twenty as in highte.
> Foure of the clokke it was tho, as I gesse,
> For ellevene foot, or litel moore or lesse,
> My shadwe was at thilke tyme, as there,
> Of swiche feet as my lengthe parted were
> In sixe feet equal of proporcioun.
> Therwith the moones exaltacioun,
> I meene Libra, alwey gan ascende,
> As we were entring at a thropes ende;
> For which oure Hoost, as he was wont to gye,
> As in this caas, oure joly compaignye,
> Seyde in this wise: 'Lordynges everichoon,
> Now lakketh us no tales mo than oon.'

> *With that the Manciple ended his tale.*
> *The sun had sunk from the meridian*
> *so far that, to my view, it had*
> *no more than twenty-nine degrees altitude.*
> *It was then, I guess, four o'clock,*
> *for eleven foot, more or less,*
> *was my shadow's length at that time,*
> *in proportion to my length*
> *in a ratio of eleven to six.*
> *Furthermore the moon's position in the sky*
> *within the constellation Libra, was steadily rising,*
> *as we reached the edge of a village;*
> *and so, our Host, since he was used to direct,*
> *our merry company, as he did on this occasion,*
> *said this: 'My lords, one and all,*
> *now there is just one tale left to be told.'*

▶ How does Chaucer suggest in these lines that this is a moment of gravity and significance? Is the mention of the sign of Libra important?

Nevertheless, and unlike some of his contemporaries, such as Langland, Chaucer cannot be labelled as a poet who thunders home a moral message. The work of the Russian critic, M. M. Bakhtin, as it relates to Chaucer, is discussed in Strohm's *Social Chaucer* (see page 110) and Peggy Knapp's *Chaucer and the Social Contest* (1990). Bakhtin saw two sides to life and literature, which he called Lent and Carnival – official behaviour and the rules which govern society are challenged by the spirit of Carnival, overturning, temporarily, orthodox and sober behaviour, celebrating instead the unruly, bawdy and immoral. He wrote of the language of the novel as 'the living mix of varied and opposing voices', and it is precisely this social mix of voices suggesting different ideals and attitudes that gives *The Canterbury Tales* their rich texture. The overthrow of 'official' and decorous behaviour becomes clear the moment Chaucer allows the strident, drunken Miller to insist on being heard as soon as the Knight has finished his tale. The author is signalling that the unruly, rebellious side of life will be presented, alongside conventional moral attitudes – and that he will not take sides. Certainly *The Parson's Tale*'s position in the text appears significant, and the subsequent *Retractions* by the author show a concern for the state of his own soul that makes it appropriate to believe this is Chaucer abandoning at last the many masks behind which he has hidden. But the Parson's voice is just one among many; and the *Retractions* may be simply a literary convention. We must remember that Chaucer insisted that his *Canterbury Tales* were just a 'game', for which he had no responsibility, and the prize for the best tale told would be a good meal at a pub.

Assignments

1 Present a critical appraisal of one of the passages in Part 3, applying one of the critical approaches discussed in this section. It could be valuable to work in a group, with each member of the group applying a different method of critical evaluation to the same passage.

2 How important are the questions of social frictions and/or feminist issues in any Chaucer text you know well?

3 Read a critical account of a piece of medieval writing you know well; how far do the views of the writer coincide with your own?

5 | Writing about Chaucer and his contemporaries

- How essential is a thorough understanding of the language of the text?

- How important is an awareness of genre, characterisation and theme?

- How far will your response be governed by an understanding of the text as a product of its time?

The language of the texts

Confident and informed response to medieval literature is impossible unless the reader feels comfortable with the language. It may help to begin by reading a good translation of the text you are studying but this is no substitute for returning to the original as soon as possible. Derek Pearsall writes, in *The Canterbury Tales, Studies in the Age of Chaucer* (1987):

> a moderate amount of effort and concentration, and sensible use of a good glossary, reap immediate rewards. Every line read in the original contributes to an advance in understanding; every line read in translation seals off Chaucer and his English more finally.

Initial labour allows the reader to be aware of use of language, rhyme and rhythm in a way otherwise impossible.

▶ Look back at the extract from *The Miller's Tale* in Part 3, page 91.

- What are your first impressions of the character described here? How clearly is she visualised?

- Why are the following described in such detail: her apron; the material used for her clothing; her purse; her brooch?

- Why has the writer used similes likening the sight of her to a pear tree, and the feel of her to soft sheep's wool?

- Is she a lady? How do you know?

- What is the tone of this description?

- Whose 'voice' is being heard here – the Miller's or Chaucer's?

- What attitudes to youth and to women can you discern from this passage?

Genre and characterisation

Since the texts most commonly studied for Advanced Level are Chaucer's *Tales,* it is important to establish what type of tale is being discussed. The assortment of story types is already known – but be aware of what to expect from each genre, and be prepared to ask yourself if what you read confirms these expectations. *The Nun's Priest's Tale,* for example, is an animal fable, based around a chicken coop in an old woman's yard; look back to the passage in Part 3 on page 86 and ask yourself what extra dimension the story gains through the language used to describe this poultry. *The Franklin's Tale* takes the form of a courtly romance, a Breton *lai,* and it is appropriate to include a lament by the desperate heroine in such a tale. But the absurdity of much of this lament's content and its extraordinary length, should signal to the reader that it has an additional purpose, both as an ironic comment on the character of the heroine and, possibly, as an indication that the Franklin has an insecure grasp of the genre he has adopted.

Characterisation is an important aspect of the rich texture of the writing. Sometimes the reader is invited to respond as if to a real person, at others Chaucer chooses to present a stereotypical figure. In *The Knight's Tale,* for example, Palamon and Arcite both fall in love at first sight. Emily's beauty gives them 'pain'; 'slain' by a glimpse, they suffer the pangs of love's arrows, and will die without some 'mercy' from her. We learn very little about the personalities of these two young men. Instead, Chaucer uses this stilted description to emphasise the unreality of the courtly love conventions. Apparently irrelevant detail can have considerable significance. The first introduction of the Wife of Bath, in *The General Prologue,* tells us that she is slightly deaf; not until the end of her Prologue do we learn why, by which time we have discerned a spiritual deafness that parallels her physical disability.

The complexity of the stories is achieved by the multiple voices involved. Chaucer the author hides behind his creation, Chaucer the naïve pilgrim, who in turn has described a variety of people, who then themselves create stories and characters of their own. This layering of voices allows for various levels of meaning, often satirical, critical or humorous, to be discerned simultaneously. In your assessment of a particular tale be prepared to consider the relevance of tale to teller, the extra dimension that is given by the narrator's personality, faults and ambitions.

▶ Look, for example, at the passage from *The Summoner's Tale* in Part 3, page 88. How much do you learn from this conversation about Thomas' wife and the visiting Friar? Remembering the discord between Chaucer's Friar and the Summoner who is telling this tale, what do you consider is likely to be the tone in which the Summoner is recounting the story? What would presumably be the reaction of the listening Friar? And is it also possible to grasp the attitude of Chaucer himself towards all his creations?

Frequently Chaucer's response to his characters and their stories is ambivalent. Be aware of moments in the text when a new dimension to the narrative is revealed. *The Squire's Tale,* for example, is so full of wondrous magical things that the teller is revealed as a romantic and gullible dreamer. In the context of *The Canterbury Tales* as a whole the story provides a telling contrast to his father's tale: in *The Knight's Tale* many of the values of chivalry are held up to question; his idealistic young son has not yet reached the stage of questioning any of them. *The Pardoner's Tale* both illustrates the preaching skills of a worldly man who exploits his congregation for his own financial gains and is also, shockingly and ironically, a powerful sermon against the very sin of greed that its teller possesses in such abundance – a sermon the Pardoner himself is too blind to understand.

Considering the style of narrative

Frequently a summary of the plot of a Chaucerian tale is swiftly accomplished – the story, as such, is quickly told. Chaucer's story-telling art lies in his use of digression and description, and it is important to recognise his deviations and the motivation behind them. *The Nun's Priest's Tale,* for example, contains a lengthy digression on the value of dreams and their interpretation, a learned and philosophical passage, which adds to the illusion of courtly romance that rides alongside the central beast-fable. The extended debate at the beginning of *The Merchant's Tale* between the knight, January, and his sycophantic friends, concerning the value of marriage, serves to highlight both likely problems to be faced later and the would-be groom's wilful determination to go his own way. Mention has already been made of the introduction and alteration of the Midas story in *The Wife of Bath's Tale,* and the excessive length of Dorigen's lament in *The Franklin's Tale.*

▶ Choose any one of Chaucer's *Tales* that you know well. Make a note of the occasions on which the writer deviates from the main plot, and account for those deviations and the way in which they enrich the narration.

Certain themes are repeated through several tales, seen from different perspectives in differing circumstances. In a similar way it is also possible to detect recurrent images. *The Merchant's Tale* is full of images of sight and blindness, reality and fantasy; *The Franklin's Tale* too suggests a tension between the real world of debts to be paid and promises to be kept and the fantasy world of magicians and gardens of courtly love. Appearance and reality both have a part to play in tales by the Wife of Bath and the Nun's Priest. Certain 'value' words, such as *gentil* [noble, virtuous] and *fresshe* [young, delicate] are used repeatedly, but with different emphasis, so that their use becomes increasingly satirical. Be alive to occasions when the tone of the writing suddenly changes.

▶ In *The Merchant's Tale,* Damian, a young squire, burns with love for the beautiful young wife of his old master, January. In accordance with conventions of courtly love he writes a secret love letter and then, sick with desire, takes to his bed. Make a note of all the aspects of vocabulary and behaviour in this passage which identify the narrative as a 'romance'.

> This sike Damyan in Venus fyr
> So brenneth that he dieth for desir,
> For which he putte his lyf in aventure.
> No lenger mighte he in this wise endure,
> But prively a penner gan he borwe,
> And in a lettre wroot he al his sorwe,
> In manere of a compleynt or a lay,
> Unto his faire, fresshe lady May;
> And in a purs of silk, heng on his sherte
> He hath it put, and leyde it at his herte.

> *This ailing Damian, suffering in Venus' fire of love,*
> *burnt so fiercely that he was dying of a passion,*
> *so great that his life was at risk.*
> *He could carry on in this way no longer,*
> *so secretly borrowed pen and ink,*
> *and in a letter wrote down all his misery,*
> *in the style of a complaint or a lay,*
> *addressed to his beautiful, fresh lady, May;*
> *and in a silk purse, which hung on his shirt*
> *he put this, placing it next to his heart.*

May visits the sick Damian and he secretly passes the letter to her; she hides it, and returns immediately to her husband:

> But unto Januarie ycomen is she,
> That on his beddes side sit ful softe.
> He taketh hire, and kisseth hire ful ofte,
> And leyde him doun to slepe, and that anon.
> She feyned hire as that she moste gon
> Ther as ye woot that every wight moot neede;
> And whan she of this bille hath taken heede,
> She rente it al to cloutes atte laste,
> And in the privee softely it caste.

But she returns to January,
and sits gently on the edge of his bed.
He takes hold of her, and kisses her many times,
then straight away settles down to sleep.
She pretends that she has to go
to the place everyone needs sometimes [the privy];
and when she's grasped the content of the note,
she eventually tears it into bits
and throws it down the lavatory.

▶ How does this second passage compare in tone and content with the first? What does Chaucer achieve by this juxtaposition? Is it possible to learn anything of May's personality from this?

The text as a product of its age

This book began with a comment by C.S. Lewis on the value of understanding the 'foreign country' of old books in order to appreciate them properly. It is essential underpinning to any informed and balanced assessment of medieval literature. Perceptive critical writing should both recognise and comment on contemporary issues that inform the text, and also note its relevance and significance to modern readers. Remember Chaucer and his contemporaries were writing in a world in which some things were taken for granted: the importance of the one established Christian church in the lives of all; the growing sense of a national identity; the vitality and friction of a society bursting the restraints of the old social order. These are but a few. Remember, too, Chaucer's own position: well read, close to but not intimately part of the highest social circles, a man not isolated from the world of trade and business, but one who clearly recognised and valued his work as a poet.

▶ Read the following passage from *The Pardoner's Tale,* commenting on its historical significance as a piece of fourteenth century writing, and on its value as a piece of poetry to be appreciated today:

Thise riotoures thre of whiche I telle,
Longe erst er prime rong of any belle,
Were set hem in a taverne for to drinke,
And as they sat, they herde a belle clinke
Biforn a cors, was caried to his grave.
That oon of hem gan callen to his knave:
'Go bet,' quod he, 'and axe redily
What cors is this that passeth heer forby;
And looke that thou reporte his name weel.'
'Sire,' quod this boy, 'it nedeth never-a-deel;

It was me toold er ye cam heer two houres.
He was, pardee, an olde felawe of youres;
And sodeynly he was yslain to-night,
Fordronke, as he sat on his bench upright.
Ther cam a privee theef man clepeth Deeth,
That in this contree al the peple sleeth,
And with his spere he smoot his herte atwo,
And wente his wey withouten wordes mo.
He hath a thousand slain in this pestilence.'

These three rioters of whom I speak,
long before prime had been rung by any church bell,
were sitting in a tavern drinking,
and as they sat they heard a bell clinking
carried before a corpse being taken to its grave.
At this one called to his servant boy:
'Go quickly,' he said, 'and ask right away
whose body it is that's passing by here;
and be sure you get the name right.'
'Sir,' said the boy, 'there's no need for that;
it was told me two hours ago before you arrived.
He was, by God, an old companion of yours;
killed suddenly, during the night just gone,
completely drunk, as he sat up on his bench.
There came a stealthy thief, that men call Death,
who kills all the people in this country,
and who split his heart in two with his sword,
and went on his way without a word.
He has destroyed thousands in this cursed plague.'

Assignments

1 How would you define the qualities of knighthood, chivalry and *gentillesse?* How are these satirised or applauded in any one (or two) of the following works: *The Knight's Tale, The Merchant's Tale, The Wife of Bath's Tale, The Clerk's Tale, The Franklin's Tale?*

2 In your reading of Chaucer, what evidence do you find of individuals challenging their accepted role in society?

3 Choose two of Chaucer's *Canterbury Tales* in which the views of women as temptress Eve and/or virtuous Mary are held up for examination. What does Chaucer say about these stereotypes?

4 Choose an extract from a piece of medieval writing by an author other than Chaucer to compare and contrast with a passage you know well by Chaucer himself. (You can, of course, use a passage from this book, but might enjoy further research. You will find the website: http://www.luminarium.org/lumina.htm particularly fruitful, giving access to works by Gower, Langland, the Gawain poet and many others, including anonymous medieval lyrics and medieval plays.)

5 Is it possible to enjoy Chaucer's *fabliaux* as anything more than bawdy knockabout humour?

6 Working in a group, or individually, present a reading and interpretation of one of the passages from Part 3. Explain the following aspects: the literary context; the historical and social context; the vocabulary; the identity and 'voice' of the speaker; the overall significance of the passage.

7 How strongly do you feel Chaucer is representing the conventional views of the society of his day? Is he in any sense rebelling against them? You may wish to do some historical and literary background research to justify your answer. Some of the books and websites listed in the Resources section will be helpful here.

8 Working in a group, draw up your own anthology of medieval literary highlights, containing passages from texts you have encountered. Justify your choices.

9 How far is Chaucer a comic writer? How serious are his underlying views?

10 If you were asked to justify the continued reading of Chaucer and other medieval authors by both students of English Literature and the general reading public, how would you go about it?

6 | Resources

Further reading

Critical works

- Helen Cooper *The Canterbury Tales,* Oxford Guides to Chaucer (Oxford University Press, 1991)
  Succinct, informative and readable, this book contains summaries of all the tales and *The General Prologue,* as well as critical readings, and an overview of the complete text. It is enormously helpful.

- Jill Mann and Piero Boitano eds. *The Cambridge Chaucer Companion* (Cambridge University Press, 1998)
  Helpful essays on a variety of Chaucerian texts, in particular *Troilus and Criseyde* and *The Canterbury Tales,* by scholars including Strohm, Pearsall and Spearing.

- J.J. Anderson ed. *Chaucer: The Canterbury Tales* Casebook Series (Macmillan, 1992)
  Critical essays from twentieth century scholars and earlier writers.

- Janette Dillon *Geoffrey Chaucer; Writers in their Time* (Macmillan, 1993)
  Discusses Chaucerian texts simply and clearly, emphasising the importance of the historical background to the subject matter.

- Jill Mann *Chaucer and Medieval Estates Satire* (Cambridge University Press, 1973)
  Influential and instructive work about the medieval class system.

- Jill Mann *Geoffrey Chaucer* (Harvester Wheatsheaf, 1991)
  A reading of the tales which offers a feminist slant.

- Derek Pearsall *The Life of Geoffrey Chaucer, A Critical Biography* (Blackwell, 1994)
  Useful insights into both the life and the works of the poet.

- Steve Ellis *Chaucer at Large* (University of Minnesota Press, 2000)
  Clearly traces the critical approaches to Chaucer in the last two centuries.

Background reading

- Barbara Tuchman *A Distant Mirror* (Papermac, Macmillan, 1995)
  Historical background information; exceptionally well written, detailed and wide-ranging.

- Keith Harrison (trans.), Helen Cooper ed. *Sir Gawain and the Green Knight* (Oxford University Press, 1998)
  Contains a very useful introductory section.

- Beadle and King eds. *York Mystery Plays* (Oxford University Press, 1995)

- Eileen Power *Medieval People* (Dover 2000) and *Medieval Women* (Cambridge University Press, 1997)
  Relevant and detailed and lively.

- Terry Jones *Who Murdered Chaucer?: A Medieval Mystery* (Methuen 2002)
  Presents a provocative new slant on Chaucer's role in society by suggesting that he was murdered for political reasons in 1400.

Novels with a medieval background are increasingly available. Two books which provide insight into the medieval mind are William Golding's *The Spire,* published by Faber, and Barry Unsworth's 1992 Booker Prize winning *Morality Play.* Anya Seton's novel *Katherine,* published in 1954, about Chaucer's sister-in-law, the wife of John of Gaunt, is helpful on background detail. More recently, a series of novels by Candace Robb, centred on medieval York in the late fourteenth century, is well researched with explanatory notes on issues such as church law.

Websites

The number of websites devoted to Chaucer and medieval writers in general indicates the interest in this period, particularly in American universities. These are some of the most useful:

- http://www.luminarium.org/lumina.htm
  Biographical notes and excerpts from texts by Chaucer, Julian of Norwich, Gower, the *Gawain* poet; medieval plays and medieval lyrics; essays (mostly by students), medieval music and images. A clear and entertaining starting point.

- http://etext.virginia.edu/mideng.browse.html
  Extracts from *Sir Gawain,* comparison between the work of Sir Thomas Malory and Chaucer; medieval lyrics.

- http://geoffreychaucer.org
  Takes you to a useful and annotated guide to a variety of online resources, including biographical information, commentary, images and historical background.

Other resources

It is very helpful to know what medieval literature sounds like when read aloud by experts, and *The Wife of Bath's Tale, The Miller's Tale* and *The Merchant's Tale* are all available on cassette from Cambridge University Press.

A series of animated cartoons based on *The Canterbury Tales,* directed by Jonathan Myerson and shown on BBC television 1998–2000, gives some idea of the basic tales, but omits much important detail.

The Knight's Tale is a film made in 2001 in which 'Geoffrey Chaucer' has a bit part. Worth watching if only for the dynamic tournament scene near the beginning.

A series of television plays shown in autumn 2003 offered interesting modern interpretations of several of *The Canterbury Tales.*

Some key dates

Century	Important events	Landmarks in English literature	Literature abroad
Pre–1000			
Late 5th century	Several invasions of England by Angles, Saxons & Jutes		
7th century	Northumbria Christianised	Caedmon's poetry	
		731 Bede's *Historia Ecclesiastica Gentis Anglorum*	
1000–1100			
		*c.*1000 *Beowulf* in Old English	
1066	Norman invasion of England		
1090s	First Crusade		
1100–1200			
1170	Becket murdered in Canterbury		1160–90 Marie de France writes Breton *lais*
1190	Third Crusade		1170–90 Chrétien de Troyes writes courtly love poetry
1200–1300			
1215	Magna Carta		*c.*1230 *Roman de la Rose* begun by G. de Lorris
		1235 William of Ockham born [d.1349] influential theologian	1265 Dante Alighieri born [d. 1321]
			*c.*1280s *Roman de la Rose* completed by Jean de Meun
1300–1400			
Crusades peter out (but pilgrimage boom lasts for some time)			1304 Francesco Petrarch born [d.1374]
			*c.*1304–21 Dante's *Divine Comedy*
		1330 William Wyclif born [d.1386]	1313 Giovanni Boccaccio born [d.1375]
1337	Beginning of 100 Years War between France and England	*c.*1330 John Gower born [d. 1408]	1349 Boccaccio's *Decameron*
1348	Black Death reaches England	*c.*1343 GEOFFREY CHAUCER born [d.1400]	*c.*1364–1430 Christine de Pisan writing ballads and *lais*
1377	Death of Edward III: minority of Richard II	*c.*1370 Chaucer's *Boke of the Duchess*	
1378	The Papal Schism – Papal authority badly shaken	1375–80 Langland's *Piers Plowman*	
		1370–80 *Sir Gawain and the Green Knight*	
1381	The Peasants' Revolt	*c.*1374–78 Chaucer's *House of Fame*	
		1379 John Trevisa translates *Polychronicon* from Latin	
		*c.*1380 Chaucer's *Parlement of Fowles*	

Some key dates

Century	Important events	Landmarks in English literature	Literature abroad
		c.1380–1400 Wyclif's Bible	
		c.1381-6 Chaucer's *Troilus and Criseyde*	
1389	Richard II assumes full sovereignty	c.1387 Gower's *Confessio Amantis*	
1399	Deposition of Richard II Accession of Henry IV	1387–1400 Chaucer's *CANTERBURY TALES*	
1400–1500		1400 GEOFFREY CHAUCER DIES	
1401	Statute for burning heretics	1412–20 Lydgate's *Troy Book*	
1413	Henry V succeeds his father	1413 Julian of Norwich *Revelations (complete copy)*	
1413	Renewed fears of spread of Lollardry		
1415	Henry defeats French at Agincourt	1413 Margery Kempe begins her visionary career	
1420–22	Henry proclaimed heir to French throne	1425 First surviving letter of the Paston family	
1422	Normandy under English rule; Henry VI becomes king		
1429	Joan of Arc leads French resistance	1425–50 John Shirley copies works of Chaucer	
1453	Henry VI suffers nervous collapse and subsequent loss of regal authority		
1455	Beginning of civil war between Yorkists and Lancastrians		
		1470 Malory's *Morte d'Arthur*	
		1476 William Caxton sets up printing press in Westminster	
1485	Battle of Bosworth – death of Richard III. Accession of Henry VII, first Tudor king		

Glossary

alliterative verse poetic form deriving from Old English depending for effect on using several words beginning with the same letter in each line

apocryphal of doubtful authenticity

Breton lay (or *lai*) romantic story told or influenced by poetry of Marie de France

caesura rhythmic break or pause in the middle of a verse line

clerk a literate man, often, not always, a church official

courtly love term devised in the nineteenth century to summarise the chivalrous and romantic behaviour celebrated and later satirised in much medieval literature

estates satire criticism of all classes of society which revealed the gap between the ideal and the actual behaviour of each group

fabliau (pl.-x) a comic, often vulgar, tale about ordinary people in a contemporary setting

franklin wealthy landowner not descended from aristocratic forbears

gentillesse a term summarising all the qualities required of a truly noble person

iambic pentameter a line of verse containing ten syllables, with alternate syllables (second, fourth etc.) being stressed. Most of *The Canterbury Tales* are written in this form.

indulgences dockets, giving Papal authority for the purchaser to obtain remission from punishment after death for sins committed

Lollard a follower of Wyclif, who challenged accepted church beliefs and practices

octosyllabic line of verse containing eight syllables

Papal Schism period during which more than one bishop claimed the title of Pope

proem introduction or prologue

rhyme royal seven line stanza poetic form, associated with courtly subject matter, deriving from French poetic form

vernacular common native language of a country

Index